Twayne's United States Authors Series

EDITOR OF THIS VOLUME

Kenneth Eble

University of Utah

Don Marquis

TUSAS 393

Don Marquis

DON MARQUIS

By LYNN LEE
University of Wisconsin-Platteville

TWAYNE PUBLISHERS
A DIVISION OF G. K. HALL & CO., BOSTON

Copyright © 1981 by G. K. Hall & Co.

Published in 1981 by Twayne Publishers,
A Division of G. K. Hall & Co.
All Rights Reserved

Printed on permanent/durable acid-free paper and bound
in the United States of America

First Printing

Frontispiece photo of Don Marquis courtesy of
Wide World Photos, Inc.

Library of Congress Cataloging in Publication Data

Lee, Lynn.
Don Marquis.

(Twayne's United States Authors series; TUSAS 393)
Bibliography: p. 155–61
Includes index.
1. Marquis, Don. 1878–1937—Criticism and interpretation.
PS3525.A67Z76   813'.52   80-20007
ISBN 0-8057-7282-0

To Mary, Matthew, and Meredith

Contents

About the Author

Lynn A. Lee, born and raised in South Dakota, graduated from Augustana College with a major in English. After completing an M.A. degree at the University of South Dakota, he earned a Ph.D. in American Studies at the University of Minnesota. He has taught at Auburn University, Alice Lloyd College and, since 1966, at the University of Wisconsin-Platteville.

Preface

From 1915–1930, it would have been difficult to find an American humorist who was any better known than Don Marquis. Yet, in the more than forty years since his death, Marquis's reputation has nearly disappeared. Today, if Marquis is recognized at all, it is as the creator of Archy and Mehitabel—a fate Marquis himself predicted. While it would be foolish to claim literary greatness for Don Marquis, it is equally foolish to ignore him. He produced a small body of humorous and non-humorous writings that can still be enjoyed and are of surprisingly high quality.

This study has two main purposes. The first is to introduce the reader to the almost unknown and very substantial body of Marquis's work. Since Marquis worked in nearly every genre, I have divided the book into chapters dealing with each one individually. Chapter 1 is a brief sketch of Marquis's life; Chapter 2 deals with Marquis as a columnist, the role in which he was best known to many Americans; Chapter 3 discusses Archy and Mehitabel, his best known creations; Chapter 4 is about The Old Soak and Hermione, two of his most successful comic characters; Chapter 5 deals with Marquis the poet; Chapter 6 discusses his novels; Chapter 7 examines his short stories; Chapter 8 is about his plays; Chapter 9 deals with Marquis's unclassifiable humor; Chapter 10 examines Marquis's lifelong interest in cosmic questions; and Chapter 11 evaluates Marquis's contribution to American humor, and his stature as an American humorist.

The second purpose of this book is to make a case for Marquis as a major American humorist. I cannot fully agree with Christopher Morley's view of Don Marquis as a modern Mark Twain, a view I will deal with more fully throughout the book; however, I do believe that Marquis, as much as any modern American humorist, did use the techniques of classic American humor to produce memorable twentieth-century humor.

I discovered Don Marquis over twenty years ago by reading my brother's copy of *Archy and Mehitabel.* At that time, I had no interest in reading any of his other work. Only gradually, through teaching courses in American humor, did I come to read more of Marquis. I would hope that this study of him will encourage the reader to go beyond *Archy and Mehitabel* to discover the many other rewards of reading Don Marquis. If this happens, my labors will have been rewarded.

LYNN LEE

University of Wisconsin-Platteville

Acknowledgments

I should like to thank the following for permission to quote from copyrighted material.

J. B. Lippincott Company for excerpts from "O Rare Don Marquis" and "A Successor to Mark Twain" by Christopher Morley. Copyright 1939 by Christopher Morley, in *Letters of Askance* published by J. B. Lippincott Company. Used by permission.

Houghton Mifflin Company for excerpts from "Amost Toujour Gai" by Bernard DeVoto. Copyright 1950 by Bernard DeVoto, in *The Easy Chair* published by Houghton Mifflin Company. Used by permission.

Doubleday & Company, Inc., for Introduction by E. B. White from *The Lives and Times of Archy and Mehitabel* by Don Marquis. Copyright 1950 by Doubleday & Company, Inc. Reprinted by permission of the publisher. Excerpts from *O Rare Don Marquis* by Edward Anthony. Copyright 1962 by Edward Anthony. Reprinted by permission of Doubleday & Company, Inc. From *The Almost Perfect State* by Don Marquis. Copyright 1917, 1918, 1919, 1920, 1921 by Sun Printing & Publishing Association, copyright 1922, 1923, 1924, 1925 by New York Tribune, Inc. From *The Dark Hours* by Don Marquis. Copyright 1924 by Doubleday & Company, Inc. From *Sonnets to a Red-Haired Lady and Famous Love Affairs* by Don Marquis. Copyright 1922 by Doubleday & Company, Inc. From *Sons of the Puritans* by Don Marquis. Copyright 1939 by Doubleday & Company, Inc. From *Sun Dial Time* by Don Marquis. Copyright 1921, 1928, 1929, 1930, 1934, 1935, 1936 by Don Marquis. From *A Variety of People* by Don Marquis. Copyright 1929 by Don Marquis. From *Off the Arm* by Don Marquis. Copyright 1930 by Don Marquis. From *The Old Soak's History of the World*. Copyright 1924 by Doubleday & Company, Inc. From *The Lives and Times of Archy and Mehitabel*. Copyright 1927, 1930, 1933, 1935, 1950 by Doubleday & Company, Inc. From *Chapters for the Orthodox* by Don Marquis. Copyright 1921 by D. Appleton Century Co., Inc., copyright 1934 by Don Marquis. From *Archy and Mehitabel* by Don Marquis. Copyright 1927, 1930 by Doubleday & Company, Inc. *All Reprinted by permission of Doubleday & Company, Inc.*

I am grateful to the staff of the Karrmann Library, University of Wisconsin-Platteville for assisting me in securing the library materials needed.

Finally, this acknowledgment can in no way give my wife, Mary, the credit she deserves for playing such a large part in the making of this book.

Chronology

1878   July 29: Born in Walnut, Illinois, to Dr. and Mrs. James Stewart Marquis.

1893–   Works, without great success, at various jobs, including writing
1899   a column for county newspapers.

1898   Attends Knox College in Galesburg, Illinois, for a few months.

1900–   Works on newspapers in Washington, D.C., and Philadelphia.
1902

1902–   Works for the *Atlanta News* and the *Atlanta Journal*
1907

1907–   Works for J. C. Harris's *Uncle Remus's Magazine*. Marries
1909   Reina Melcher on June 8, 1909.

1909–   Free-lance writer in New York City.
1912

1912   *Danny's Own Story* (novel). Originates "The Sun Dial" column in the *New York Evening Sun*.

1915   November 7, Robert Stewart Marquis (only son) born.

1916   First appearance of Archy and Mehitabel in "Sun Dial," March 29. *The Cruise of the Jasper B.* (novel).

1917   *Hermione and Her Little Group of Serious Thinkers* (humorous sketches).

1918   Barbara Marquis (only daughter) born.

1919   *Prefaces* (humorous sketches).

1921   February 15, Robert Stewart Marquis dies. *Carter and Other People* (short stories). *The Old Soak* (humorous sketches). *Noah an' Jonah an' Cap'n John Smith* (poetry).

1922   *The Old Soak* runs for 423 performances on Broadway. *Sonnets to a Red-Haired Lady and Famous Love Affairs* (poetry). *The Revolt of the Oyster* (short stories). Begins writing "The Lantern" for the *New York Herald Tribune*.

1923   December 2, Reina Marquis dies suddenly.

1924   *The Old Soak's History of the World* (humorous sketches). *The Awakening and Other Poems* (poetry). *The Dark Hours* (drama).

1925   Gives up writing a daily column.

1926 February 2, marries Marjorie Vonnegut. *The Old Soak* (drama).

1927 *Archy and Mehitabel* (humorous sketches). *The Almost Perfect State* (utopian humor). *Out of the Sea* has a very brief run on Broadway.

1928 *Love Sonnets of a Caveman* (poetry). *When the Turtle Sings and Other Unusual Tales* (short stories). Begins his sporadic career as a screen writer in Hollywood.

1929 Heart attack. *A Variety of People* (short stories).

1930 *Off the Arm* (novel), *Everything's Jake* is produced in New York without much success.

1931 October 26, Barbara Marquis dies.

1932 November 14, *The Dark Hours*, directed by Marjorie Marquis, opens on Broadway to a very brief run.

1933– *Archy's Life of Mehitabel* (sketches). *Master of the Revels*
1934 (play). *Chapters for the Orthodox* (humorous sketches).

1935 *Archy Does His Part* (humorous sketches). *Master of the Revels* is produced at Union College in an outdoor setting.

1936 February, Marquis suffers a third stroke, affecting his speech and sense of locomotion. Works on *Sons of the Puritans*. October 25, Marjorie Marquis dies suddenly.

1937 December 29, Marquis dies.

CHAPTER 1

"Don Marquis—What Is He?"[1]

DURING his lifetime, Donald Robert Perry Marquis (as in -uiss) did not suffer from a lack of friendly criticism. He was praised as a columnist, a poet, a short story writer, a novelist, and, to a lesser degree, as a dramatist. Unfortunately, today, more than four decades since his death, only his most famous work, *Archy and Mehitabel*, is recognized by even a small part of the American reading public, fulfilling his own prophecy that he would be remembered, at best," . . . for creating a cockroach character."[2]

Since Marquis's death, there have been some attempts to renew interest in his work. In the 1940s Christopher Morley, Marquis's friend and greatest booster, edited an anthology of Marquis's writings.[3] In the 1950s E. B. White and Bernard DeVoto wrote favorable criticisms of his work.[4] In 1962 Edward Anthony published *O Rare Don Marquis*, a lengthy biography. Although Anthony is unselective, making little attempt at critical analysis of Marquis's work, he does reprint large parts of Marquis's unpublished "egobiography" and numerous other documents relating to Marquis's life and work, particularly his early years. Anthony also includes many anecdotes about Marquis's drinking problem, his many friendships, his membership in the Players Club, and his family problems.

In discussing Marquis's life, I have drawn heavily on Anthony's biography, but I have avoided Anthony's uncritical approach, emphasizing the three elements contributing most to his development as a writer: his boyhood in Walnut, Illinois; his wandering arrival as a successful newspaper columnist; and, finally, the personal tragedies he suffered as a husband, father, and brother, culminating in his own decline and early death.

I   *From Walnut to the World*

In Marquis's unpublished "egobiography," he makes his birth nearly cosmic in importance by stating that he was born during an eclipse of

15

the sun. Whether or not Marquis was born during the actual eclipse, in his own mind it marked him as one who would leave Walnut far behind and become famous.

Since Marquis used Walnut for the setting of various works, some idea of what it was like in the late nineteenth century is essential. *The Walnut Centennial Book,* published in 1972, gives one a clear impression of life in Walnut in the late 1800s. As photographs testify, it was a typical midwestern small town, centering around the railroad depot, the businesses on the main street, and, most important, the rich farmland surrounding the town.[5]

Marquis's father, Dr. James Stewart Marquis, came to Walnut after the Civil War. A lover of nature, unlike his son, Dr. Marquis also had a rather extensive library which his son used frequently, as can be seen in much of his work.

Although remembering Walnut after nearly a forty year absence made some stretching of the truth inevitable, Marquis realized that much happened there when he was a boy. For example, in his "ego-biography" he recalls a murderer who was converted while in prison and became a pillar of the Walnut Baptist Church. Experiences such as this helped Marquis form deep suspicions about religion.

As a boy of ten, Marquis spent approximately a year in Chicago, where his mother was operating a boarding house near the University of Chicago, and his sisters were attending the university. Marquis remembered being in Chicago on the day the Haymarket bombers were hanged, and being told by a schoolmate that the anarchists had threatened to blow up the city if their comrades were hanged.

After returning to Walnut, Marquis worked at various jobs during the mid and late 1890s: while working in a drug store, he created a spectacular explosion while playing with chemicals; while working as a chicken-plucker, his experiences were so vivid that he later thought of immortalizing them under the title "The Memoirs of a Feather Yanker; or It's Pluck That Counts." It was at this time that Marquis claims he started writing poetry under the influence of Darwin and Carlyle, composing "The God-Maker Man," although with a different title.

In the fall of 1898, Marquis attended Knox College in Galesburg, Illinois. He left, according to his own account, because he couldn't play football and work his way through college at the same time. He also had difficulty feeding his enormous appetite.

During the late 1890s, in addition to his brief college career, Marquis

was a country schoolteacher and a railroad section hand before taking
a job on a weekly county newspaper. At no extra pay, he produced a
column featuring numerous stories he claimed to have invented about
Lincoln. Another way of filling space was the thirteen-line sonnet. Marquis started writing such sonnets for the column because a printer's
stock could hold only thirteen lines of iambic pentameter:

So I habitually produced thirteen line sonnets. A white mule couldn't be
found dead or a three-legged calf born in that county, but that I made a song
about it. I even wrote sonnets about W. J. Bryan.[6]

Not long after Marquis wrote an editorial suggesting that the incum-
bent Republican congressman for the district ought to be replaced by
a more progressive Republican, he was offered a job with the Census
Bureau in Washington, D.C. Marquis took the job, although he always
believed that the job was offered in order to take pressure off the congressman.[7] While working at the Census Bureau, he also did some
newspaper work, but was unable to get his own column. After leaving
the Census Bureau for political reasons, Marquis briefly tried his luck
in Philadelphia, then went to Atlanta where he had been offered the
associate editorship of the *Atlanta News*, a recently formed paper. In
this position, he could write as many columns as he wanted to. In fact,
Marquis portrays himself as being so naive that he didn't mind supply-
ing free copy simply for the joy of writing a column.

II *Atlanta: The Years with Harris*

Marquis spent approximately seven years in Atlanta working for several newspapers and for *Uncle Remus's Magazine,* under the editorship of Joel Chandler Harris. In Atlanta he met, courted, and married
his first wife, Reina Melcher, a free-lance writer. Besides Reina, the
three most important people in Marquis's Atlanta life were Grantland
Rice, who was on his way to becoming the most famous sportswriter
in America; Frank. L. Stanton, probably the most famous southern
newspaper columnist in the early twentieth century; and, of course,
Joel Chandler Harris. Rice encouraged Marquis to keep trying to
become a well-known columnist; however, Stanton, a good friend of
Rice and Marquis, had such a popular charm that Marquis could in no
way compete with him.

Marquis left the *News* to join the *Atlanta Journal*. His writing there was confined mainly to editorials. On his own time, Marquis wrote a great deal of poetry which, he claimed, was thrown out as scrap paper by a janitor.

In 1907, when Joel Chandler Harris started *Uncle Remus's Magazine,* Marquis became the associate editor, in charge of the editorial pages and the book reviews. This gave him a wider range for his talents. Because the magazine had a national circulation, Marquis wrote about a wider variety of subjects, ranging from the location of Billville, an imaginary Georgia town invented by Frank Stanton, to a mildly satiric treatment of John D. Rockefeller.

Marquis also wrote parodies of popular literary forms such as the melodrama and the open-road school of poetry made popular by Richard Hovey. Probably the most significant of his prose pieces was that dealing with Upton Sinclair's plan to do research for a novel satirizing upper-class life in Newport, Rhode Island, by disguising himself as a servant. Marquis suggested that Sinclair would do better to " . . . cast aside disguises altogether" and go " . . . as a Cockroach."[8] As Hamlin Hill points out, this is the first hint of the coming of Archy.[9]

All in all, the magazine was an ideal training ground for Marquis, allowing him to speak in a wide variety of voices. If the magazine had had a long life, Marquis might well have settled permanently in Atlanta. However, after Joel Chandler Harris's death in 1908, the magazine lost a good deal of its charm. Marquis did stay with *Uncle Remus's Magazine* until late 1909, but, after a pay cut, he left.

III   *New York: The Successful Columnist*

With Reina's encouragement, Marquis left Atlanta in late 1909. He wanted to make a name for himself as a New York columnist in the vein of Franklin Pierce Adams.[10] He planned to find work in New York, then send for Reina. Through the winter and early spring of 1910, he struggled with various jobs, including free-lance writing and a job on the *New York American* as a rewrite man. The *American* also printed Marquis's own work, although not as a column.

Thinking that he had succeded in the big city, Marquis sent for Reina. In March 1910 he was fired by the *American*. According to Marquis, he and Reina went on a starvation diet for three months. In desperation, he then borrowed enough money to wire Boston, Washington, and Cincinnati for jobs. He received three offers, but Reina convinced him to stay in New York. At this point, Marquis sold an idea for a serial feature to the *Sunday Herald* and wrote 17,000 of the 20,000 words in the four installments before collapsing from fatigue. Reina finished the story, took it to the *Herald* office and collected two hundred dollars for the feature.

For the first few years they lived in New York, the Marquises supported themselves largely by free-lance writing. Both continued to sell stories and poems to *Uncle Remus's Magazine*. Marquis worked for the *New York American* again as a rewrite man, and, for a time, with the *Brooklyn Eagle*. His free-lance work ranged from a memoir of the Civil War service of the 14th Regiment, a New York unit, to a series he did for the *Herald* titled "Reveries of a Bigamist," based supposedly on the memories of a man who had been married thirteen times in twenty years.

In 1912, Marquis was given the opportunity he had been waiting for ever since his arrival in New York. He began writing "The Sun Dial" column for the *New York Evening Sun*. When writing "The Sun Dial" and after moving to the *New York Tribune*, where he wrote "The Lantern" from 1922–1925, Marquis was as well known as any columnist in New York. From the beginning, he relied heavily on the use of comic characters such as The Old Soak, Hermione, and Captain Peter Fitzurse. When, on March 29, 1916, he introduced Archy and Mehitabel to "Sun Dial" readers, he not only found the perfect voices for his views, but he, more than any other American humorist, made the daily newspaper column into a masterful comic device. Archy and Mehitabel were used in "The Sun Dial" and "The Lantern," and Marquis also made use of them, particularly Archy, when he was writing a page for *Collier's* nearly every week in the late 1920s and early 1930s. There is little hope of persuading the president or the Congress to designate March 29 as Archy and Mehitabel's birthday, but it should be remembered as the single most significant date in Marquis's long career and one of the most significant dates in American humor.

IV   Fame and Futility

By the time Marquis stopped writing a daily column in 1925, he was a well-known, popular figure. His creations—Archy and Mehitabel, Hermione, and The Old Soak—had become part of the American imagination. Certainly, anyone would have been justified in predicting a continued success for Marquis.

Even though Marquis no longer wrote a daily column in a New York newspaper, he continuted to publish stories, poems, and articles in numerous magazines. Beginning with *Danny's Own Story* (1912) and including the posthumously published *Sons of the Puritans* (1939), Marquis published twenty-six books, ranging from novels to short stories to poetry to such unclassifiable works as *The Almost Perfect State.* This does not include privately printed works which were distributed in limited editions.[11]

It would be untrue to insist that all or even many of these works are the best of American humorous or nonhumorous literature. Marquis allowed too much second-rate work to be published and republished. From the time of the publication of his first volume of poetry, *Dreams and Dust* (1914), he lamented the inferior work, especially poetry, published under his name.

Three main reasons can be found for Marquis's allowing so much inferior work to be published. The chief reason was a need for money. From approximately 1916 until his death, Marquis was the chief support of his sisters, Maud and Neva. Another reason was Marquis's apparent lack of critical acumen when it came to his own work. Even in work not written to meet a deadline or to pay pressing bills, there is unevenness. Finally, Marquis was not served well by the critics since, for the most part, they either ignored him or were very flattering.

In his continual search for new sources of income, Marquis spent considerable time in Hollywood during the late 1920s and early 1930s. He went there originally in the hope that the warm climate would be good for his daughter Barbara who was in poor health. During this visit, in the winter of 1928 and the spring of 1929, he did some writing, and met some movie people, but apparently did not make any serious attempts to get work with a studio. He returned to New York with Maud, Neva, and Barbara via the Panama Canal, in the late spring of 1929. This first visit to Hollywood gave Marquis the inspiration for one of his weakest works, *Off the Arm* (1930), a superficial novel, redeemed only, if at all, by a few satirical touches.

Throughout the next few years, Marquis took short-term work in Hollywood for three to four months at a time. George Middleton, a playwright who knew Marquis in Hollywood, believed no one was very sure how to use Marquis's talents.[12] Marquis even insisted that he overheard two drunks at a Hollywood party who weren't even sure how to pronounce his name.

Despite this lack of stature, Middleton believed that Marquis could have been a successful screenwriter.[13] He also mentions that Marquis was amused at the inability of Hollywood to use writers at their best. Marquis was not allowed to write screenplays for Will Rogers, although both men were satisified with such collaboration. He was not allowed to write the screenplay for *Kim*, a book he read yearly.[14] Like many other writers, Marquis found Hollywood impossible to conquer or even meet on equal terms. Yet, he kept returning to work for studios— largely because the money was good. For example, in 1931 he worked for nineteen weeks at $1,500 a week. Despite the financial rewards, Marquis was never able to become a successful screenwriter. He believed he was unsuccessful because he couldn't tolerate bad writing.

Marquis never fully recovered from his daughter Barbara's death in Hollywood in 1931. From that time on, he was not happy in Hollywood, although he did work there, off and on, until 1936. By 1936 Marquis's increasingly bad health made him anxious to complete *Sons of the Puritans*. Also, by 1936, Hollywood did not have a great deal of interest in Marquis.

On the whole, Marquis's Hollywood experiences were not happy ones. They did yield one inferior novel, at least one good short story, and one unpublished poem. Yet, like so many other gifted writers of the time, Marquis found himself stymied by a supposed art form that resisted using artists at their best.

Marquis's last years were the culmination of many years of frustration and personal tragedy. Besides the financial problems involved in maintaining a home for his two sisters and providing for his own family, Marquis was involved a good deal of the time in arguments with his sister, Maud. Maud did not get along well with either of her sisters-in-law. Neither did she function very successfully as an aunt. Whether or not, as some have claimed, Maud was a drug addict, she was certainly one of the chief sources of frustration in Marquis's life (Anthony, 339–340).

Besides the financial and personal problems brought on by Maud, Marquis also suffered a number of personal tragedies. His only son, Robert Stewart Marquis, died in 1921 at the age of five. Reina Marquis died suddenly in late 1923. His only daughter, Barbara, died in 1931 at the age of thirteen. In 1936, approximately one year before her husband's death, Marquis's second wife, Marjorie, also died suddenly. Those closest to Marquis felt that he never totally accepted his son's death, and the loss of his daughter and wives added greatly to the already present grief.

Marquis's own health was not good for the last part of his life. In January 1929 he suffered a severe heart attack while living in Hollywood. In November 1932, shortly before the opening of *The Dark Hours*, Marquis's drama of the Crucifixion, he suffered what some doctors called uremic poisoning, others a vascular disturbance.

In February 1936 Marquis suffered a third stroke. From this time until his death on December 29, 1937, he was virtually incapable of doing any sustained work, even by dictation. Throughout 1936, Marquis's condition worsened. By the spring of 1937, he was nearly totally helpless, unable to speak more than a few words and unable to read except at a very slow rate. By the last few months of his life, doctors had given up the slim hopes they had for his recovery. Marquis was reduced to lying helplessly while a few of his friends would visit him briefly. His death came as a relief to all who had watched him suffer for so long.

Because of his tremendous suffering and loss of artistic power, many of Marquis's friends saw him as a tragic figure. Besides the many newspaper and magazine obituaries, which were filled with praise for Marquis the man and Marquis the artist, Benjamin DeCasseres, a close friend, published a brief eulogy, using the book of Job as a framework. In DeCasseres's version, God orders Satan to strip Marquis of " . . . all he hath in the manner of Job."[15] When Satan asks why since he can think of no evil deeds done by Marquis, God (called the Great Impresario) states that Marquis had committed the unpardonable sin: "a sense of humor touching things sacred and divine."[16] DeCasseres then summarizes what happens to Marquis:

And so that man Don, in the land of America, who was upright and eschewed evil and who was beloved of all men and who gave to his last, *had his son taken from him, and then his wife, and then his daughter, and then he was stricken blind, and then he had his second wife taken from him, and then he was paralyzed, and then his speech was taken from him, and then his mind was darkened, and then he was paralyzed again*—and thus, utterly helpless and stricken, *his properties and moneys were drained from him, and he lay in great agony and weakness* until the Great Impresario and his man Satan, seeing that no further evil could be done unto Don, who was upright, eschewed evil, who was beloved of all men and who gave to his last, sent his soul into the Valley of the Shadow.[17]

In the second part of the eulogy, Marquis is brought before the Great Impresario and asks the Great Impresario why he has done this to him.

God cannot reply; instead, he " . . . grew gray on his throne and Satan shriveled up like a man of a thousand, thousand years."[18] At this point, the Angels of Laughter fill the heavens, insisting that Marquis has created the Kingdom of Cosmic Mirth, "The Laughter that topples gods from their thrones, and against that none shall prevail."[19] In a concluding vision, Marquis becomes a triumphant figure: " . . . his soul was carried into the Valhalla of Triumphant Mirth, where he shall reign as a shining spiritual presence while there still lives on Earth a single man or woman who knew DON MARQUIS."[20]

Whatever the literary merits of this eulogy, it does suggest the great love Marquis received from his many friends in the journalistic world, at the Players Club where he was a longtime member, and from many people he came into contact with. The eulogy presents Marquis as a humorist on a spiritual level, a view which combines the two contradictory sides of Marquis the man and Marquis the artist. Today, more than forty years after his death, the details of Marquis's life have been nearly forgotten. He is remembered, if at all, as the creator of Archy and Mehitabel. Yet, as I hope to show in the following chapters, Marquis left a small but substantial body of humorous and nonhumorous work, besides his greatest work, *Archy and Mehitabel*, that deserves far greater recognition than it has received.

CHAPTER 2

Marquis as Columnist: "The Twenty-Three Inch Grave"

I "Where the Hell's That Column of Yours?"

THROUGHOUT most of his career, Don Marquis had a love-hate relationship with writing a daily column. Although he developed Archy and Mehitabel, The Old Soak, Hermione, and other humorous characters in his column, his strong dislike of producing a daily column can be seen when he talked about his request to be released from his contract with the *New York Herald Tribune*, in 1925. "I got to seeing my column as a grave, twenty-three inches long, into which I buried a part of myself every day—a part that I tore, raw and bleeding, from my brain."[1] Later, he remembered both hating and loving "the column-writing" game:

... I can look back upon the 13 years when I was chained to a column—like the well known Prisoner of Chillon ... while it ruined me, I loved it. ... I am apt to walk into any newspaper office in America at any hour of the day or night and hand in half a dozen columns if I don't watch myself, and give them away for nothing but the pleasure of seeing them in type. I loathe, hate, abhor and dread the column-writing game. I think of it as the most poisonously destructive vice to which any writer may become addicted ... and at the same time I love it and adore it and yearn for it and have to fight against it.[2]

In fact, Marquis's love of writing a column was so great that, in 1933, he began publication of a four-page daily paper, written entirely by himself, to be called the *Column*. However, although one issue was printed, it was never distributed.

Early in his career, Marquis had formed very definite ideas about the format of a successful column. When he was young, he read Eugene Field's column, "Sharps and Flats," and George Ade's column,

24

"Stories of the Streets and of the Town," and, when working in Atlanta, had known Frank N. Stanton, the most popular southern columnist of the early twentieth century. By the time he got his own signed column in New York, he was ready to put some of his views into practice:

A column must have plenty of white space, a challenging make-up, constant variation in typographical style; not only must it catch the eye but it must have points and corners and barbs that prick and stimulate the vision, a surface and a texture that intrigue and cling to and pull at the sight. . . . I tried to get as much variety in the stuff itself as there was in its typographical presentation. So, besides the verse, paragraphs, sketches, fables and occasional serious expression of opinion, I began to create characters through whom I might comment upon or satirize current phases of existence, or whom I might develop for the sheer pleasure of creation.[3]

Although Marquis was very careful about all aspects of his column, there were times when his guidelines would be forgotten. As he tells it, he would be enjoying himself in Lipton's, a favorite newsman's bar, with Christopher Morley and other friends when a copy boy from the newspaper would arrive with an ultimatum:

"Mr. Marquis, it's only an hour before that page has gotta be locked up, and the foreman he says, where the hell's that column of yours. . . . Ain't you wrote it at all yet? . . . he says some of these days you're gonna look at the paper and wonder why you ain't in it!"[4]

At such times, Marquis wrote his column rapidly, with the help of contributors.

During his best years as a columnist, which were also the best years of the personal newspaper column in America, Marquis was recognized as one of the best columnists in a field that included such distinguished men as Franklin P. Adams, always known as F. P. A., and Heywood Broun and Christopher Morley. In 1923, Carl Van Doren saw Marquis as better than his fellow columnists because there " . . . is a racy substance in him which makes him able to create characters as no one of the others can."[5] Van Doren finds that Marquis possesses the special gifts a columnist must have to practice his art.

For example, a reader of Marquis's column "The Lantern," during the weeks of March 19 to June 14, 1924, when he had been writing a column for almost a decade, would have been exposed to much of Marquis's serious and humorous skill as a columnist and a writer. In the columns for these three months, nearly all the familiar characters are found, in addition to parody, nonsense, guest contributors (a group which all columnists relied on to fill the column on days when they were not inspired or had a copy boy at their heels), and serious touches—the variety which Marquis believed made up a successful column.

However, even when Marquis relied on contributors, it was, apparently, difficult for him to stay out of the column. For instance, the first half of the May 15, 1924, column is a comic reaction to a reader's protest of Marquis's treatment of the New Testament. Marquis had said, "The New Testament came along because God was getting a little bit cramped in The Old Testament."[6] Following this are two poems, one lyric, one comic, both by contributors. Marquis surrounds the poems with a few one-line aphorisms such as "Pity the meek, for they shall inherit this earth."[7]

II   Safe Targets

Besides the varied format and the superb comic characters, Marquis relied on poking fun at rather safe targets to make his column popular. Of the targets available, none was safer than politics. Marquis tried to steer a course between the two national parties, pointing out shortcomings on both sides, while leaving a general impression of politics being irrational and unsavory, a view that has been safe for American humorists since the early days of our nation.

In 1924, the Teapot Dome scandal would have been an irresistible political target for any columnist—humorous or nonhumorous. Marquis used it in various ways during the early part of 1924. On April 26, "The Lantern" featured a chapter of an imaginary novel, *Thicker Than Blood*, by Earl Barrington Sinclair. This is "a new serial of intrigue in the capitols of the world and the love of strong men for clean women by the author of 'The Great Gland Mystery,' 'Man! Man!,' 'Lady! Lady!,' 'The Body in the Desk,' 'The Crimson Crime,' 'Fingerprints in Blood,' etc."[8] Here, as in other burlesque novels found in his columns, Marquis is making fun of melodramatic serialized novels and detective stories, but he is also poking fun at Teapot Dome. The hero of *Thicker Than Blood* is Rupert Thackaway, the youngest United States senator, who is gathering evidence about "the oil-well scandal" in a " . . . House on K Street."[9] Since members of the so-called

"Ohio Gang" operated from "The Little Green House" at 1625 K Street,[10] Marquis's target would be obvious to most of his readers.

Besides using Teapot Dome in *Thicker Than Blood,* Marquis used it when referring to a convention orator nominating " . . . a decrepit old moron . . ."[11] because he was the only man in the United States who has not been subpoenaed. In another column, Marquis portrays the chairman of a Senate committee grilling a witness who saw a season baseball pass being delivered to the White House by a messenger who was later killed in an accident. Marquis did not take sides in Teapot Dome, but tried to see the comic aspects of both sides. He took the always acceptable view that no politician of either party should be completely trusted or taken seriously. Undoubtedly, readers in 1924 welcomed any sort of comic relief from Teapot Dome just as readers in the 1970s welcomed Art Buchwald's columns on Watergate.

On a more biting level, Marquis responds to the news that the governor of Indiana has just gone to jail and would resign as governor with the suggestion that " . . . just as soon as a politician takes office, send him to jail for the entire term of his office."[12] If the politician does a good job, he could be released when his term expires; if not, keep him in jail. The only problem with this scheme is a possible debasement of " . . . the moral tone of our prisons."[13]

Since 1924 was a presidential election year, Marquis offered what he titled A PLATFORM FOR ALL PARTIES. In an obvious parody of party platforms which try to appeal to all members of the party and as many voters as possible, he offers these planks: taxes should be reduced, but revenue should be raised; new laws should be enacted from time to time; when convenient, the United States should have a foreign policy; "The military and naval establishment of the country should be at times reduced and at other times expanded."[14] Finally, on the matter of religious and social toleration, he suggests a plank which would be welcomed by everyone:

All religions and races should be tolerated, from time to time, here and there, if necessary, although the parties signatory to this declaration expressly affirm that this matter of toleration is not a matter of general policy, but of local option.[15]

While finding humor in politics is not difficult, finding humor in crime would not seem so easy. Yet, Marquis is able to get considerable

humor from crime. He devotes one entire column, March 19, 1924, to
one, a series of "Letters to a Great-Grandson." In this particular letter,
he attempts to explain the crime wave or waves of the 1920s. Marquis
believes it is easy for " . . . the acute and patient crook" to rise into
respectability and power in modern America:

The population is so vast, the machinery of business and government is so
enormously intricate and complicated, that it is impossible for the great
majorities who are stupid and inclined to be halfway honest, to keep track of
the clever crook's activities.[16]

Approximately one week after "Letters" appeared, Marquis devoted
"The Lantern" to a less serious view of crime, ridiculing the treatment
of women bandits who " . . . are operating in Brooklyn and New York
. . . if one of them gets caught, the cold eye of the camera will probably
show her up as a sharp-faced weathered jade long past her flapping
teens."[17] Anticipating the era of Bonnie and Clyde, Marquis uses this
opening to ridicule "Sunday Editors" who glamorize any woman connected with crime.[18] As in many other columns, he uses an anecdote
from his own past experiences, telling of how he was present, fifteen
years earlier, when a female outlaw was arrested in Tennessee:

She was said to be young and beautiful—the tale of her beauty spread over
three counties; in no time at all it was a Golden Legend. Personally, we were
all het up about her, ready to fall in love with her . . . to rescue her from the
militia and the sheriff's posse.[19]

When the "Girl Bandit" appears, romance vanishes:

She was a discouraging looking hag well past fifty, with blackheads in her
nose and with dirty fingernails. Moreover, she used a snuff stick; and if you
have ever seen a woman use a snuff stick, you will at once become uninter-
ested in her. . . .[20]

By contrasting romantic illusion with reality, a favorite device of
American humorists, Marquis, indirectly, is asking the reader to laugh
at himself for ever believing what a "Sunday Editor" presents as the
truth. Not content with debunking the modern "Outlaw Lady," Marquis reinforces his point: "It is very probable that Maid Marian had

two front teeth gone, big feet, a squint and chronically uncombed hair."[21] The problem, as he sees it, is that men are always searching for the perfect "Outlaw Lady"; however, if they do find a young woman who seems to fit this ideal, they will not want her to be the mother of their children. At the conclusion of the column, Marquis reverts to the opening. The police will capture the Girl Bandit with one of two results:

Either she turned into a cross moll because some wicked gonoph made her, or else she has snaggle teeth. The snaggle teeth will make no difference to the Sunday Editors, however; the captions and cut lines will, as usual, call attention to her milky youth and divine pulchritude.[22]

III   *"Pages"*

Although Marquis never returned to writing a daily newspaper column after 1925, in the early 1930s he wrote a column of sorts for the *Saturday Review of Literature*. Also, he wrote a "page," as he called it, for *Collier's* with off-and-on regularity from the late 1920s to the mid-1930s. When one examines these *Collier's* "pages," it is obvious that Marquis thought of them as columns. The vast majority of them are similar to "The Sun Dial" and "The Lantern," making heavy use of Archy and Mehitabel and The Old Soak. A typical *Collier's* "page" would begin with a comment by The Old Soak concerning Prohibition or the Depression, then would include a note from Archy and a few comments in Marquis's own voice. Marquis did, in some cases, devote the entire column to Archy, but not often.

While most of the *Collier's* "pages" use familiar material and situations, they are still entertaining. One of the funniest is The Old Soak's version of *Hamlet*, called "What Happens to Grouches."[23] The Old Soak sees Hamlet as a grouchy prohibitionist who never drinks. He kills "Polinarius" because of a grudge; he jilts Ophelia, causing her to commit suicide. He is angry at the "Two Jewish fellows" named "Rosenberg and Guildenstein," and has them framed by some racketeers down by the waterfront. The Old Soak thinks Hamlet is probably happy at the end of the play, even though he is dying, because of all the bodies littering the stage. Hamlet gets what he deserves: "Sooner or later a grouch will get what he has been laying up for himself."[24]

Another of the "pages," written in 1926, is worth mentioning because of its treatment of war. In "If You Know What I Mean," Marquis describes how war will be changed by the late twentieth century.[25] In 1985, Germany declares war with France

... and instantly puts 85,000 men—the full force allowed by the League of Nations to a country of a total population of 85,000,000—into the field. France sent forth 40,000 men against these troops ... the League had permitted Great Britain ... to come to the assistance of France with 50,000 soldiers. The men fought with the arms permitted by the League of Nations— swords, spears, maces, battleaxes, daggers, bows and arrows, slings.[26]

Marquis sees the League of Nations as having enough power to regulate the ways in which wars will be fought, supporting itself by charging a 10 percent royalty for licensing wars. Armies are almost totally volunteer except for "compulsories." This last group consists, in each country

... of all politicians and statesmen who had voted for war, or who had spoken for war, as well as all editors and orators who had demanded that the martial bowows be unleashed for the glory and honor of the nation and the advance of civilization. The volunteers were all unmarried, young, romantically inclined—and of course patriots as well. Many of them went into politics in their thirties, and did very well at it too.[27]

The League's control of war will be very popular since it will not force people opposed to war to pay for one. Also, by returning to ancient weapons of war, the cost of armaments will drop drastically. While Marquis's plan isn't perfect, it will work in a transitional period.

When one reads Marquis's columns, even over the period of a few weeks, it is not difficult to see the reasons for his great popularity. His skill in varying the format of his column, of using the characters he created for the column with maximum effect, made "The Sundial," "The Lantern," and his magazine "pages" justifiably popular.

In Marquis's columns, one can see nearly all aspects of his writing that are found in his other works: his great skill in creating humorous characters, his ability in burlesquing popular literary forms, his use of the humorous story and comic verse, his ability to interweave humorous and nonhumorous views of the same topic, his distrust of most institutions and those who control them, and, finally, his preoccupation with "cosmic" questions. If these sound like qualities common to other

American humorists, particularly Twain, that is exactly what was intended. In his columns, Don Marquis carried on the traditions of native American humor in the twentieth century.

The best way to sum up what Don Marquis accomplished as a columnist is to simply restate what E. B. White said of Marquis:

I think the new generation of newspaper readers is missing a lot that we used to have, and I am deeply sensible of what it meant to be a young man when Archy was at the top of his form and when Marquis was discussing the Almost Perfect State in the daily paper. Buying a paper then was quietly exciting, in a way that it has ceased to be.[28]

CHAPTER 3

"The Creator of a Goddam Cockroach"

DON Marquis has survived as a humorist because of Archy and Mehitabel, two of the most famous characters in American humor. At present, the first of three Archy and Mehitabel books, *Archy and Mehitabel*, is in paperback, and a hardbound edition of the three Archy and Mehitabel books, *Archy and Mehitabel, Archy's Life of Mehitabel*, and *Archy Does His Part*,[1] continues to sell very well. Marquis believed, somewhat unhappily, that he would be remembered only as "the creator of a goddam cockroach" (Anthony, 410). It is unjust to Marquis to remember him only in this way; yet, Archy and Mehitabel are his greatest creations, representing an almost perfect use of earlier American humorous techniques to deal with a twentieth century urban environment.

I   *The Arrival of Archy*

While Archy's actual origin will never be known for certain, a friend of Marquis's remembers a day when he and Marquis went to Lipton's, a favorite newspapermen's bar. While they were splitting a bottle of champagne, Marquis said, "Frink, this morning there scampered across my desk the goddam biggest cockroach you ever saw. I believe he could damn near play my typewriter" (Anthony, 142). While this moment in Lipton's may have been Marquis's first thought of using Archy in his column, several years earlier, while working for *Uncle Remus's Magazine*, Marquis wrote as column for January 1908 which included a paragraph entitled "Literary Cockroaches." As mentioned in the first chapter, in this paragraph Marquis discusses the rumor that Upton Sinclair is writing a novel to expose Newport society based on Sinclair's experiences in the homes of the wealthy disguised as a servant. Marquis does not find this the best solution:

Of course there was another way open to him; if it was absolutely necessary for his literary purposes to crawl around the kitchen sinks of other people, to

32

pry into their wardrobes, to scramble along their pantry shelves, to scurry from under their beds, and so forth, he might have cast aside disguises altogether and gone as a cockroach.[2]

Hamlin Hill sees this as " . . . the germinal conception of Archy, the roach who, as Marquis explained in 'the ballade of the under side' had an important function in offering information and opinions from this novel point of view."[3]

When Marquis introduced Archy in "The Sun Dial" on March 29, 1916, he gained considerable freedom as a columnist. As E. B. White suggests, it allowed Marquis to fill space rapidly with short lines without having to worry much about such things as punctuation and capitalization.[4] Marquis immediately established an uneasy relationship with Archy. Marquis never allowed himself to become totally fond of Archy and Mehitabel, resisting Archy's demands for greater credit, more pay and better food to the extent that one of the longer sustained episodes in *Archy Does His Part* deals with a strike by Archy and the negotiations which follow. By making him a cockroach, the most common urban insect, Marquis gives Archy a universal quality:

We came into our room earlier than usual in the morning and discovered a gigantic cockroach jumping upon the keys. . . . He would climb painfully upon the framework of the machine and cast himself with all his force upon a key, head downward, and his weight and the impact of the blow were just sufficient to operate the machine, one slow letter after another. . . . After about an hour of this frightfully difficult literary labor he fell to the floor exhausted, and we saw him creep feebly into a nest of the poems which are always there in profusion.

Congratulating ourself that we had left a sheet of paper in the machine the night before so that all this work had not been in vain, we made an examination and this is what we found:

> expression is the need of my soul
> i was once a vers libre bard
> but i died and my soul went into the body of a cockroach
> it has given me a new outlook upon life
> i see things from the under side now . . .
> there is a cat here called mehitabel i wish you would have
> removed she nearly ate me the other night why dont she
> catch rats that is what she is upposed to be for
> there is a rat here she should get without delay
> most of these rats here are just rats

but this rat is like me he has a human soul in him
he used to be a poet himself
night after night i have written poetry for you
on your typewriter
and this big brute of a rat who used to be a poet
comes out of his hole when it is done
and reads it and sniffs at it
he is jealous of my poetry
he used to make fun of it when we were both human
he was a punk poet himself
and after he has read it he sneers
and then eats it . . .

that rats name is freddy
the next time freddy dies i hope he wont be a rat
but something smaller i hope i will be a rat
in the next transmigration and freddy a cockroach
i will teach him to sneer at my poetry then . . .
leave a piece of paper in your machine
every night you can call me archy (20–21)

From the beginning of the Archy and Mehitabel saga, the tone is established: Archy's continual shifting between humility and pride, Mehitabel's unreliability. Making Freddy the Rat a critic is the perfect touch since he is able to eat what he doesn't like—the perfect criticism. Even though Archy disagrees with Freddy's criticism of Archy's poetry, it is clear from the beginning that Archy was not a very good poet when human and that, if anything, becoming a cockroach has given him a greater view of the world, if not a greater talent.

When Marquis was writing "The Sun Dial" with Archy, they could rely on such current topics as reincarnation and free verse; however, if he had not been able to establish Archy and Mehitabel as memorable humorous characters, it is doubtful that the books would be read today by a mass audience.

Of the two, Mehitabel's character is more clearly defined since she is an uncomplicated open spirit; whereas, Archy reveals himself more gradually. From Archy's first message, we learn that he is a poet, sensitive to criticism, sensitive about his stature, and that he is not materialistic; in fact, he wants little more than a few bread crumbs. Archy works very hard at being an artist, but expects no reward except the bare necessities of life and the freedom to create. If this sounds like the picture Marquis drew of himself as an eager young columnist, who would write columns without being paid, it is no accident. The combination of romance and cynicism found in Archy's work fits much of Marquis's work very closely, particularly his fascination with so-called "cosmic philosophy." Archy's character is developed largely through his views instead of his actions which consist basically of roaming the city, seeing the world from the underside. It is hard to imagine a more insignificant being than Archy; yet, he does not feel inferior to man having mainly contempt for most human behavior and for the behavior of the nonhuman world.

II *"Toujours Gai"*

If Archy is the artist encased in a roach's body who feels superior to much of his current environment, Mehitabel makes few distinctions between individuals in her pursuit of love and life. Her motto, "toujours gai," reflects the flapper philosophy of the post–World War I era, but also reflects the uninhibited, freedom-loving side of American culture found in earlier American humor.

Mehitabel's character is largely developed in *Archy and Mehitabel*. (By the time of *Archy Does His Part*, she appears for only a brief interlude.) Marquis establishes her character almost immediately; everything that follows is a variation of "toujours gai" or her less refined, more American version of the same sentiment, "wotthehell." By giving Mehitabel a song which she sings, with slight variations, throughout her existence, Marquis vividly and permanently immortalizes Mehitabel:

> i have had my ups and downs
> but wotthehell wotthehell
> yesterday sceptres and crowns
> fried oysters and velvet gowns
> and today i herd with bums
> but wotthehell wotthehell
> i wake the world from sleep
> as i caper and sing and leap
> when i sing my wild free tune
> wotthehell wotthehell
> under the blear eyed moon

> i am pelted with cast off shoon
> but wotthehell wotthehell . . .
>
> i know that i am bound
> for a journey down the sound
> in the midst of a refuse mound
> but wotthehell wotthehell
> oh i should worry and fret
> death and i will coquette
> there is a dance in the old dame yet
> toujours gai toujours gai (23–24)

The use of slang and such rhymes as "moon" and "shoon" permit the reader to take Mehitabel comically. Yet, the linking of "toujours gai" with a trip down the Sound on a garbage scow adds a note of realism, making Mehitabel a universal character.[5]

Although Archy worries considerably about Mehitabel, wishing that she would settle down, or, at least, be more sedate, he also gets vicarious enjoyment in listening to Mehitabel tell of her adventures, which generally involve sex and violence. In this sense, Mehitabel is a throwback to earlier frontier humor which dealt openly and freely with violence, and, to some degree, with sex. Mehitabel is an individual, refusing to compromise with society, even if it would mean an easier life; she accepts the fact that she will end up on a garbage mound.

The combination of fatalism and hedonism makes Mehitabel's life, itself, poetic. As a humorist, Marquis did not make this point too seriously. Mehitabel lives for the moment. Nearly all her adventures take a similar form: contact with a member of the opposite sex, declaration of true love, a lyric interlude, a rather violent parting, and, too often, another litter. However, throughout these passages, Mehitabel insists on being treated like a lady. She is not interested in marriage, motherhood, or middle-class responsibilities. She sees marriage as a threat to her art, leading to "one dam kitten after another" (216). Anyone attempting to explain Mehitabel's popularity must avoid the temptation to make her too profound. She functions as the perfect foil for Archy, the sensitive cockroach, who cannot accept "toujours gai" as the guiding motto for a happy or productive life. Mehitabel's dancing with Boreas, her refusal to give up her bohemian life and accept middle-class security, her acceptance of death, all are qualities not normally thought of as comic. Yet, since these qualities are embodied in an alley cat, the incongruity makes Mehitabel a superb comic creation.

III   *Poet of the Under Side*

As a cockroach, the most common urban creature, Archy cannot be expected to live his life as poetically as Mehitabel. In fact, he shows little interest in being "toujours gai," resisting the advances of a lady-bug and other female insects, while continually brooding over Mehitabel's casual attitude toward life, love, and death. Archy's character is dominated by this desire to create, to leave his art with the world, and his sense of frustration at being trapped in the body of a cockroach:

> gods i am pent in a cockroach
> i with the soul of a dante
> am mate and companion of fleas
> i with the gift of a homer
> must smile when a mouse calls me pal
> tumble bugs are my familiars
> this is the punishment meted
> because i have written vers libre
> . . .
> i with the brain of a milton
> fell into the mincemeat at christmas
> and was damned near baked in a pie
> i with the touch of a chaucer
> to be chivvied out of a sink
> float through a greasy drain pipe
> into the hell of a sewer
> i with the tastes of a byron
> expected to live upon garbage
> gods what a charnal existence
> . . .
> i with the soul of a hamlet
> doomed always to wallow in farce (73–74)

The use of Dante, Chaucer, Homer, and Byron, the idea of a poet being a mouse's pal, or the idea of falling into the mincemeat make Archy's lament comic; obviously, he is not to be seen primarily as heroic.

While there is little sustained narrative, Marquis does move Archy through a varied existence which resembles, at least superficially, the life of an artist-intellectual in the twentieth century. If Archy were only a vers libre poet, he would have little depth. However, besides being a poet, Archy is, at various stages of his career, a would-be

reformer, a radio commentator, a Washington correspondent, a world
traveler, a prude, an anarchist, and, as previously mentioned, a dweller
on the underside of life. Throughout all of these roles, Archy fluctuates
between humility and vanity. He is particularly vain when he is full of
self-pity.

With so much vanity, Archy is also a bug of the masses, continually
on the alert for mistreatment of those other creatures on his level of
existence. He is, of course, not complacent about being a roach of the
underside, as seen in "ballade of the under side":

> the roach that scurries
> skips and runs
> may read far more than those
> that fly
> i know what family skeletons
> within your closets
> swing and dry
> not that i ever
> play the spy
> but as in corners
> dim i bide
> i can t dodge
> knowledge
> though i try
> i see things from
> the under side (249)

As can be seen, Archy is a cynic. There is a sinister tone in the references to family skeletons and hiding in corners. However, the major
point is Archy's dislike of pomposity and the inability of the pompous
to hide from Archy. As a result of his underside observations, Archy
finds no basis for man's claims of superiority over insects:

> and i never saw a city
> full of men manage to be as happy
> as a congregation of mosquitoes
> who have discovered a fat man
> on a camping trip (207)

By reducing Archy's preference for insect society to a one-line joke,
Marquis keeps a humorous tone while retaining the idea that man has
neither intelligence nor appreciation of beauty and is unlikely to

acquire either. While the steady decline of humanity is assured, there are still battles to be fought, standards to be upheld.

Two of the most important words Archy will fight for are "anarchy" and "beauty." It is tempting to connect Archy's anarchism to Marquis's being in Chicago at the time of the Haymarket bombers' execution. Yet, when Archy declares his anarchism, one cannot take it that seriously:

> you thought i was only
> an archy
> but i am more than that
> i am anarchy
> where have i been you ask
> i have been organizing the insects
> the ants the worms the wasps
> the bees the cockroaches
> the mosquitoes
> for a revolt against mankind (188)

His desire is to organize the insects, to overthrow the ruling class. Yet, one can also read Archy's outburst as tall talk, the attempt of the underground or frontier hero to assert his importance. Since he is only a cockroach, one can also read the whole assertion as comic.

IV   *The View from the Under Side*

Through Archy, we can, if we desire, accept a world in which insects will dominate when things are set aright. Yet, Archy does not limit his criticism of vain and stupid behavior to human beings. In the course of recounting his adventures, Archy frequently indulges in fables to make a point. Some of these represent Marquis at the top of his form as a humorist. In "warty bliggins, the toad," Marquis describes a toad who believes that he is the center of the universe. Archy cannot resist questioning Warty about his views:

> . . . to what act of yours
> do you impute
> this interest on the part
> of the creator
> of the universe
> i asked him

        why is it that you
        are so greatly favored

        ask rather
        said warty bliggens
        what the universe
        has done to deserve me
        if i were a
        human being i would
        not laugh
        too complacently
        at poor warty bliggens
        for similar
        absurdities
        have only too often
        lodged in the crinkles
        of the human cerebrum (57)

Within the space of a few lines, using only a cockroach, toad, and toadstool, Marquis satirizes man's self-centeredness. It is the microcosm that
makes the satire effective since, within his very narrow perception,
Warty may be correct. If the world is a toadstool, the rest follows.
Archy appears to take Warty Bliggens seriously until the conclusion of
the fable when he refuses to let mankind feel superior to Warty. The
humor comes from the pompous language and self-assurance of a toad,
with the not very subtle reminder that men are only toads on a larger
scale.

    If Archy can find one thing of value in a vain world, not about to be
reformed by insects, it is beauty, particularly beauty created by an artist. Although Archy knows he is incapable of evoking beauty except
through his art, he wrestles with the problem of how to live for beauty
in "the lesson of the moth." In this fable, Archy becomes very middle
class, referring to the moth's desire to die for beauty as "a stunt." He
also reminds the moth that it makes little or no sense to be burned to
death for beauty. The moth replies:

        it is better to be happy
        for a moment
        and be burned up with beauty
        than to live a long time
        and be bored all the while (95)

Archy connects man and moth when the moth insists that its attitude of "come easy go easy" is what human beings believed "before they became too civilized to enjoy themselves" (96). "Enjoyment" is a key word for Archy and Marquis; throughout his work, Marquis insists that the more civilized man becomes, the less he enjoys life.

Being on the underside, Archy is able to observe the more mundane ways in which man attempts to find enjoyment. His opinions on drinking, the theater, and other diversions are interspersed throughout the Archy and Mehitabel trilogy.

Since Marquis himself was given, at times, to overindulgence, it is not surprising that Archy falls victim to demon rum; at one point, he falls into an egg nog at Christmas and makes some rather vainglorious statements as a result. However, the most effective comic treatment of drinking links insects with the ever-popular temperance literature of the nineteenth and early twentieth centuries. In "the dissipated hornet," Archy tells of meeting a drunken hornet who relates the story of his innocent childhood, spent in stinging schoolchildren on the village green. Then he fell victim to the lure of the city, where he survived through the guidance of a worldly-wise hornet who teaches him to catch drunken flies. The hornet goes on to relate how he grew more and more victimized by drink, to the point of recruiting six innocent young hornets to catch flies for him. Unfortunately, the recruits have left him; he is now faced with a nearly tragic dilemma:

> . . . i have to catch my flies myself
> and my months of idleness and
> dissipation have spoiled my technique i
> cant catch a fly now unless he is dead drunk
> what is to become of me alas the curse
> of alcoholic beverages . . . (133–34)

Archy responds to the hornet's tale of woe by getting into a safe place inside the typewriter and telling the hornet to commit suicide since Archy's sympathies are with the flies.

In this story, besides the obvious digs at prohibition and temperance literature, Marquis uses the image of the city as the playground of Satan, a belief long accepted by rural Americans. The hornet is the hick who wanders to the city and is corrupted. The view of the pastoral life he once led is what a hornet should be in a state of natural innocence. Here, Archy, who, except for art and beauty, is not fond of excess, sympathizes with the real victims, the flies. Of course, what makes the story successful as humor is Marquis's mixture of slang, melodramatic rhetoric, frontier-type boasting by the hornet, and the rather unexpected ending.

Besides drink, another way in which Archy saw humans enjoying themselves was while attending the theater. Since Marquis was well aware of the problems of producing a Broadway hit, and since Archy saw the theater from the underside, it is really not surprising to find Archy discovering that even Shakespeare was frustrated by the public's insatiable desire for entertainment. This is clearly established in Archy's conversation with Pete, the parrot who knew Shakespeare. For the first time, the real Shakespeare is revealed to the world through a conversation between Shakespeare and Ben Jonson that Pete remembers:

> here i am ben says bill
> nothing but a lousy playwright
> and with anything like luck
> in the breaks I might have been
> a fairly decent sonnet writer
> i might have been a poet
> if i had kept away from the theatre
> yes says ben i ve often
> thought of that bill
> but one consolation is
> you are making pretty good money
> out of the theatre . . .
>
> . . . any mutt can write
> plays for this london public
> says bill if he puts enough
> murder in them what they want
> is kings talking like kings
> never had sense enough to talk
> and stabbings and stranglings
> and fat men making love
> and clowns basting each
> other with clubs and cheap puns
> and off color allusions to all
> the smut of the day oh i know
> what the low brows want
> and i give it to them (102–104)

Shakespeare's lament for his misused talent comes close to Marquis's own complaint about being remembered only as the author of "a goddam cockroach" and Archy's wailing about his insignificance. Pete's account of Shakespeare's conversation with Ben Jonson does suggest that it is possible to write for a popular audience and still create great art, something Marquis was unable to do with any consistency. Certainly, Marquis could not have treated Shakespeare so informally or so perceptively in a critical essay.

From his underside view, Archy also finds much to criticize about the United States. Besides a dislike of human behavior in general, Archy is suspicious of the government and politicians. On his first visit to Washington, D.C., during a hot July, Archy is very unimpressed:

> . . . in the
> capitol building there
> is no attention paid to me
> because there are so
> many other insects
> around . . . (248)

This is hardly an original view since Washington, D.C., the government, and politicians have been fair game for humorists from the beginning of the nation. It is not until *Archy Does His Part,* the third volume of the trilogy, that Archy emerges as a critic of the New Deal and a student of world affairs. Archy's strongest attack on the New Deal comes in an interview with Marquis. Basically, Archy finds too many experts in the administration, but he has no solutions for the problems of the country, knowing only that civilization is a failure.

Since Archy sees no future for civilization, no form of government and no world leader will have much effect. To Archy, "communism" and "democracy" are only words, just as people are only something to eat. Not until Archy, himself, feels slighted does he make an attempt to fight back. Archy's strike and the complex negotiations that follow are a mock-heroic version of the battles between labor and management that were common during the early part of the twentieth century.

As the heavy-handed boss, Marquis refuses to compromise with Archy on such demands as a helmet to avoid callouses on his brain from hitting the typewriter keys. Instead, Marquis brings in another cockroach named Henry to write the column. Although he is threatened by Archy and beaten by another cockroach, Henry is, at least, willing to attempt to learn punctuation. As a scab, Henry's treatment fits into the pattern of labor agitation in the 1920s and 1930s. As the strike progresses, it reaches mock-epic proportions:

We were informed today by an excited friend that he had seen thousands and thousands of cockroaches, led by Archy, hiding by the curbstones picketing this district, and that it seemed to him that they were maddened by benzine or something. (343)

Marquis goes so far as to threaten to hire strikebreakers, including a dozen tarantulas, to protect the contributors to his column. After more rhetoric, Marquis and Archy reach a settlement, giving Archy most of his demands, including a pint jar of plum preserves with bread and butter and all the fixings once a week.

V *The Man behind the Cockroach*

Archy gains most of his demands since Marquis needs his unique point of view to present his criticism of human nature and the particular foibles of American civilization. Through Archy, Marquis very skillfully uses various humorous techniques, such as the fable, comic verse, epigrams, parody, and some elements of frontier humor. One of the best examples of how Marquis employs earlier American humor is in Archy's account of the death of Freddy the rat, killed by a boastful tarantula who also dies in the battle:

> . . . he [the tarantula] would stand in
> the middle of the floor and taunt
> us ha ha he would say where i
> step a weed dies do
> you want any of my game i was
> raised on red pepper and blood i am
> so hot if you scratch me i will light
> like a match you better
> dodge me when i m feeling mean and
> i don t feel any other way i was nursed
> on a tabasco bottle if i was to slap
> your wrist in kindness you
> would boil over like job and heaven
> help you if i get angry give me
> room i feel a wicked spell coming on (43–44)

Archy's final comment on the battle connects older techniques with current issues:

> . . . both are no more please
> throw a late edition on the floor i want to
> keep up with china we dropped freddy
> off the fire escape into the alley with
> military honors (44)

Here, Marquis expands frontier boasting and violence into a humorous comment on world war. Keeping up with China and burying a rat with military honors are incongruous, but both reflect the fascination with violence Archy and other observers of the American scene have noted.

In another of Archy's encounters with fellow insects, Marquis again uses the flair for exaggeration so beloved by Americans. An old cockroach, who claims to have been to hell, describes it vividly:

> . . . he says he crawled into a yawning
> cavern and suddenly came on a
> vast abyss full of whirling
> smoke there was a light
> at the bottom billows
> and billows of yellow smoke
> swirled up at him and
> through the horrid gloom he
> saw things with wings flying
> and dropping and dying they veered
> and fluttered like damned
> spirits through that sulphurous mist (33)

Besides the use of overstatement and exaggeration, Marquis is fond of the epigrammatic sentence, collecting these under various titles: "maxims of archy," "archy says," "archygrams," all featuring pointed remarks, generally about human foibles. For the most part, Archy attacks fairly obvious or common targets:

> did you ever
> notice that when
> a politician
> does get an idea
> he usually
> gets it all wrong (260)

Possibly the best known of these epigrams expresses the paradox of
Prohibition aptly:

> prohibition makes you
> want to cry
> into your beer and
> denies you the beer
> to cry into (52)

I find the best humorous use of the epigram when Archy deals with
his fellow insects. Although he still does not say anything very original,
the point of view makes for a degree of freshness. With one curt obser-
vation, Archy destroys man's feeling of being the favorite of the gods:

> i once heard the survivors
> of a colony of ants
> that had been partially
> obliterated by a cow s foot
> seriously debating
> the intention of the gods
> toward their civilization (54–55)

In this brief adventure, as in "warty bliggins," Archy manages to
destroy pretentiousness, satirize those who believe that the universe has
meaning and, once again, remark on the continual ability of human
beings to see almost any event as relating to their own particular situation. However, because of the use of ants and a cow's foot, the situation is almost ludicrous. Marquis scattered these epigrams and vignettes
throughout the Archy and Mehitabel trilogy. They fit perfectly into
the columns where they originally appeared and they were also the
ideal form for a vers libre poet-cockroach who found it difficult to produce work of any great length.

While Marquis wrote and published much serious poetry, I find him
more original and successful as a comic poet. His skill as a comic poet
is most noticeable in the songs of Mehitabel:

> it s kicks or money
> life s too dam funny
> it s one day sunny
> the next day rain

> life s too dam funny
> for me to explain
> . . .
> thank god i m a lady
> and class will tell
> you hear me sadie
> thank god i m a lady
> my past is shady
> but wotthehell
> thank god i m a lady
> and class will tell
> . . .
> i never sing blue
> wotthehell bill
> believe me you
> i never sing blue
> there s a dance or two
> in the old dame still
> i never sing blue
> wotthehell bill (86–87)

It is funny for a supposed lady to use "wotthehell" and other vulgarities. The use of obvious rhymes that could be easily found in popular songs also gives a tone of lightness that contrasts with Mehitabel's somewhat dubious insistence on her perpetual dignity. Marquis intends her to be a lady and a tramp. When Mehitabel meets Bill, her new true love, she expresses her joy vividly and comically:

> for i am a lady who has her whims
> no tom cat holds my love
> if i come to feel i have plighted my troth
> to a little mauve turtle dove
>
> but at least i have found my real romance
> through the process of trial and error
> and he is a ribald brute named bill
> one eyed and a holy terror
>
> his skull is ditched from a hundred fights
> and he has little hair on his tail
> but the son of a gun of a brindled hun
> is undubitably male (448)

The rejection of "love" and "turtle dove" prepares the reader for Bill, who is unidealized but very vital. We don't get Archy's view of Bill; in fact, Archy records the song with no comment. Mehitabel will not settle down. Her constant fidelity to "toujours gai" as a way of life is not enough for Archy. Yet, by giving it so vividly, Marquis makes Mehitabel live as a memorable comic character.

One other humorous technique used effectively by Marquis is parody. Besides his parody of temperance literature and melodrama in "the dissipated hornet," Marquis parodies melodrama, with particular emphasis on the role of the mother, in "pity the poor spiders." The mother spider, left by a wandering husband who has been lured off by a centipede, is now frustrated in her attempts to provide for her family by the swatters which destroy her food supply:

> curses on these here swatters
> what kills off all the flies
> me and my poor little daughters
> unless we eats we dies
>
> only a withered spider
> feeble and worn and old
> and this is what
> you do when you swat
> your swatters cruel and cold (28)

This captures the pathos of melodrama, songs about Mother, and, generally, the sentimentalism surrounding mother and child which has pervaded American culture.

Generally, the use of Archy as a vers libre cockroach might, in itself, be considered a parody of sentimental, popular poetry. Marquis did write some effective free verse poems, but he basically used traditional rhyme and meter. As for individual poets, Archy had nothing good to say about many of them. At one point, Archy becomes "elevated" after eating a lot of Kipling's earlier poetry in a secondhand book store. Upon returning to Marquis's office, Archy launches into a parody of Kipling:

> the cockroach stood by the mickle
>   wood in the flush of the astral dawn
> and he sniffed the air from the hidden
>   lair where the khyber swordfish spawn . . . (192)

Marquis sees in Kipling's poetry the same overstatement and excessive rhetoric, with no meaning beneath the surface or even on the surface, that he found in melodrama and other forms of popular literature. Ironically, Marquis was guilty of these same excesses in his own poetry.

Archy and Mehitabel are unique, defying classification, yet, as I hope I have demonstrated, their success comes from the use of techniques common to American humor. By using these common techniques, by creating a cockroach and a cat as characters who did not need to be taken seriously and by commenting on such acceptable humorous topics as religion, politics, and human nature, Marquis was and is able to reach a vast popular audience. E. B. White sums up the immortal pair succinctly: "Archy and Mehitabel ... performed the inestimable service of enabling their boss to be profound without sounding self-important, or even self-conscious."[6]

CHAPTER 4

Beyond Cockroach and Cat:
The Old Soak and Hermione

MARQUIS'S fear that he would be remembered only as "the author of a goddam cockroach" has come true. A contemporary critic claims that Marquis " . . . is remembered almost solely for a trilogy in verse about a cockroach and a cat . . . besides scattered pieces of satire and short fiction."[1] With the exception of a very few readers, one could probably even omit "scattered pieces." Certainly, some of Marquis's works do not deserve reprinting, but a considerable part of his most successful humorous writing is virtually unknown to a modern audience. In particular, the characters of The Old Soak and Hermione await rediscovery as two of the most memorable characters in modern American humor.

I   The Old Soak

During his lifetime, Marquis created several characters who rivaled Archy and Mehitabel in popularity; the most popular was Clem Hawley, The Old Soak. He is the hero of two books, two plays, and several short stories. Clem came from "The Sun Dial," where so much of Marquis's best humor originated. He grew out of Prohibition, the great "moral experiment" of the early twentieth century, about which Marquis had very definite feelings, all negative. "He wrote almost obsessively in prose and verse against prohibition."[2]

The Old Soak is not an alcoholic; he is " . . . one whose devotion to alcoholic fellowship and endearing generosity of spirit superseded the practical concerns of work and family support."[3] Clem Hawley is much closer to the comic strip characters, Jiggs or Major Hoople, or to the character played by W. C. Fields in some of his films than he is to the drunkard of nineteenth-century melodrama. Ironically, the popularity of The Old Soak gave Marquis a reputation for being a drunk himself, a title he deserved only on infrequent occasions.

In *The Old Soak* (1921), Marquis assembled twenty-two of his many columns about Clem Hawley. Originally, Clem lives in Flatbush, but he later moves to Baycliff, Long Island, a considerably more rural area which, especially in the short stories narrated by Clem, bears a not surprising resemblance to a midwestern town such as Walnut, Illinois. Because of inherited property, Clem is able to support his family without working. He spends most of his time finding ways to acquire drinkable whiskey, reminiscing about the old time saloon, telling stories and generally enjoying himself in what he believes to be the life-style of the biblical patriarchs who Clem is sure had the only right way to live. In many ways, he is a nineteenth-century cracker-barrel philosopher and would find much in common with Josh Billings and Martin Dooley who preached using common sense and taking life pretty much as one finds it.

Because it is a collection of columns, *The Old Soak* has a loose framework. In a sense, Marquis borrows the frame, a standard device with nineteenth-century humorists, in which the author sets a meeting between the author and a humorous character and, after a brief introduction, lets the storyteller tell the story in his own style and language. In the opening chapter of *The Old Soak*, Clem visits Marquis; after warning of the dangers of home brew, he announces he is writing "A kind of gol-dinged autobiography of what me and Old King Booze done before he went into the grave and took one of my feet with him."[4] (The reference to one foot is Clem's recalling the brass rail in old-time saloons upon which one could rest one's foot.) The rest of *The Old Soak* alternates between a chapter of Clem's autobiography and a chapter in which he comments on the havoc being caused by Prohibition or on his latest domestic problems.

The Old Soak is much given to exaggerating the effects of Prohibition. Because of the bars being closed, he cannot keep up with politics or outdoor sports, since he doesn't trust the newspapers. In another chapter, Clem suggests that the next reform movement will be to take away tobacco. When this happens, there will be crime waves since many men have only tobacco to console them for the loss of whiskey. This chapter ends with Clem claiming that "the wicked" will fight back if pushed far enough. Although he is too old to fight, "I got children and grandchildren that'll fight against the millenium to the last gasp, if I know the breed, and I'm going to pass on full of trust and hope and calm belief" (OS, 20).

Another way in which The Old Soak finds Prohibition weakening the country is through a national moral decline. Clem's own moral standards are given clearly, more than once:

I never drunk nothing but whiskey for comfort and pleasure, and I never took no medicine in my life except calomel, and I always hold to the Presbyterian religion as my favorite religion because those three things has got some kick when took inside of you. (OS, 11)

Clem is suspicious of those who profess their Christianity too loudly, or, even more dangerously, spend time worrying about how good they are. "Everybody had to be good all of a sudden, and only a few had learnt how; and everybody that hadn't quite succeeded in turning Christian went around for a while wondering if everybody else was as gosh-darned Christian as they let onto be" (OS, 49). In what is obviously a parody of religious conversion and temperance literature, Clem reveals the secret of his contentment and happiness:

. . . I come right out and acknowledge Booze as my boss and master, and set him up and crowned him king, a great peace fell onto me and I been happy and contented and full of love for my fellow men ever since. (OS, 49)

Clem desires nothing more than to live his life as he wants; he has no illusions about himself or mankind. Although he cannot abide meanness, he refuses to blame Prohibition or drinking for making men mean.

Throughout *The Old Soak*, Marquis uses the clichés common to domestic humor. Clem is not unhappily married. He and Matilda have learned to tolerate one another. Yet, Prohibition forces a man to spend so much time at home that he and his wife fight. Normally, these arguments end with Clem filling his ever-present hip flask and leaving to seek consolation elsewhere.

The Old Soak blames Prohibition for creating other kinds of domestic disharmony. Now, a wife can't be sure why her husband hasn't come home, whereas before she could be sure that he had merely stopped off for a few drinks with his friends. Prohibition can also create friction over household management, as when Clem is very critical of his wife for using raisins for a pie instead of fermenting them in a cask.

The Old Soak's children are also affected by Prohibition. In a stroke of genius, he marries his daughter to a revenue agent. This assures Clem a ready supply of whiskey, since, as he puts it,

... they are always tracking down a couple thousand gallons somewhere or other, and I don't hear no glass crashin' nowheres to indicate where them bottles is bein' busted. I wants somebody in the fambly that will take me along on some of these here raids I read about. (OS, 56)

When Clem's son-in-law gets Clem's own son appointed a revenue agent, all Clem's wishes would appear to have been answered. Unfortunately, his son goes on a raid while drunk and arrests Clem's son-in-law, who is spending off-duty time in a speakeasy. This creates a split in the Hawley family between those favoring the son-in-law and those favoring the son. Since she is an ardent Prohibitionist, Matilda prays for both sides' salvation. The humor is found in the view of revenue agents who were the basis of much humor and considerable scorn during Prohibition.[5] Although both violated the law, Clem's son loses his job (he gets it back later) while his son-in-law keeps his. In neither case is there much concern with serving the government or enforcing Prohibition.

According to Hawley, since Prohibition, the country has become hard-hearted; it is no longer possible to get drunk and sing songs about home and a gray-haired mother: "And I guess them prohibitionists won't feel so smart when they see all them old ladies with grey hair flung out onto the streets in rainy weather because nobody would pay the mortgage off" (OS, 65). Here, The Old Soak provides a twist to *The Drunkard* and other temperance melodramas by suggesting that the lack of drink will destroy the America he knows and loves.

In 1924, Marquis published *The Old Soak's History of the World*, which, like *The Old Soak*, was a collection of newspaper columns. The two books are quite similar. In the second, Clem Hawley moves from discussing the old-time bar room to giving his very individualistic treatment of the Bible, ancient history, the French Revolution, and foreign culture in general, in addition to throwing in anecdotes about Baycliff, Long Island. This is certainly not an original approach for a work of humor, as it had previously been used by Mark Twain, Artemus Ward, Bill Nye, and others.

As in *The Old Soak*, Clem takes a moral stance: "You mustn't go too fur with it whatever it is."[6] If this sounds conservative, Clem balances it with another axiom:

All the histry of the old days of the world points to the fact that you better do what you want to as you go along through life for anything you do youre goon to feel later you done wrong and don't want to care too much of a dam. (OSH, 9)

This attitude makes it clear why Clem's all-time great men are the biblical patriarchs, who he sees as having cared little about anything except throwing barbeques, drinking, and having a good time.

Although Clem's interpretations give his history a distinctive tone, he is not quite as dominant a character as in the earlier book. One reason for this is that there is very little reference to his family, even to his wife. He does use a number of anecdotes about people he has known at Baycliff, Long Island, to support his interpretation of ancient history and the Bible. Concerning the latter, Clem is a "cover to cover man," reserving his greatest dislike for "a damn little athyiss" like "Hennery" Withers, a "smart alec cousin" of Jake Smith (OSH, 2). Jake owns the hotel and bar where Clem spends most of his time.

In fact, one of the chief links between The Old Soak and earlier American humor is his attitude toward the Bible, ancient civilizations, and Europe. He sees such figures as Alexander the Great, Caesar, Solomon, and Samson as being quite human with human weaknesses. Samson, for instance, was a better man drunk than many Prohibitionists would be when sober (OSH, 1). Also, like other American comic sages, Clem does not find much difference in human conduct between the past and the present:

Well they was great sports in the early days, if they got an idear they went right through with it, they uset to burn these here witches weather they done anything mean or not. Well now and then they burn a colored man in this country, but this is a republikin form of government and a man gets burned in a republikin form of government can say to his self he is geting burned for something different than in the old witch burning days and it orter be a great comfort to him to realize he is getting burned in a free country and not in one of them old countries where they was kings and tireans all ways burning people. (OSH, 35)

The link between this ironical view and Twain's treatment of modern civilization is clear. Neither is it difficult to imagine Mr. Dooley making the same point after Mr. Hennessy (Dooley's straight man) has expressed the belief that in a republic there is no tyranny of the sort found in the early days.

On the whole, the burlesque of the Bible and ancient history is not much more profound than a television skit. After one grasps Clem's basic philosophy of life, it is easy to forecast his opinion of a particular individual or event. If anything, the humor is old-fashioned for the 1920s, almost succeeding on the level of nostalgia.

Similarly, when one turns to The Old Soak's view of Europe, he finds largely traditional humor. Clem goes to France with Al the bartender; they later encounter Jake Smith, who has become quite wealthy from bootlegging. In typical American fashion, Jake has been dragged to France by his daughters who are determined to make him cultured while spending as much of his money as possible.

At first, Clem is quite content with Paris, especially after he learns how to order "cat veesky" (four whiskies) without ever learning to order less than four. He takes a great interest in French history, being particularly sympathetic toward Marie Antoinette. At one point, he believes both the Venus de Milo and Winged Victory are statues of Marie Antoinette. Clem and Al are particularly outraged at the treatment given Venus; Al gives a unique interpretation of Winged Victory when Clem tells Al, who speaks some French, to ask their "shofer" about the wings:

> Al . . . says to me the wings is to show she went to heaven in the end. Clem, he says, it is like Little Eva in Uncle Tom's Cabin; the wings is to show you can't keep a good girl down. (OSH, 90)

Later, Clem and Jake Smith are dragged to the Louvre by Al to see the *Mona Lisa*, or "Mona Lizzy" as Clem calls her. Upon viewing the portrait, each man interprets the smile differently. Jake Smith's explanation is materialistic:

> . . . she is thinking she is got a new dress on, and she is going to have still another new dress next week, and none of the other girls she knows has got two new dresses in one week, and is kind of putting it over on the other girls, and she feels pretty good about it. (OSH, 137)

Al believes " . . . she looks . . . just exactly like Herb Simpson's first wife, Nell, back in Baycliff, L. Ileland" (OSH, 137). Nell fell in love with a revival preacher and left her husband and two children. Clem takes a somewhat higher view:

You fellows ain't got any finer feelings . . . or you would see that she is thinking of something a dam site more hifaluting and refined and holy and religious than just merely duds, I am ashamed of you. . . . I seen just that same kind of look onto my own face in the mirror in Jake's bar room when the boys got a little bit soused and commenced to singing about Home and Mother. (OSH, 137)

Each view suggests the average man's fondness for reading a story or moral point into a work of art. Of course, the three interpretations are plausible; Al's, in particular, may unravel the riddle of her smile.

After spending considerable time in France, Clem, Al, and Jake become rather homesick—even though they are quite upset by having to break their country's laws in order to get something to drink. Clem's lament reflects the attitude of those who believed their virtue was greater than that of the United States: "I never knowed how much I loved my country till I realized I had lost her" (OSG, 134).

In both Old Soak books, particularly the last, Marquis indulges in one of his vices—using the same material, slightly altered, more than once. *The Old Soak's History of the World* has condensed versions of three previously published short stories narrated by Clem, while, in the same book, Clem relates a tall tale, found in both *Danny's Own Story* and *Sons of the Puritans*, describing how he fell down a well while drunk and was forced to remain in the well while the Reverend Mr. Hoskins preached an inspired revival service over him, until Clem agreed to sign the pledge for three months. Clem then announces he will pick the three months, taking one day at a time. As for the versions of the three Clem Hawley stories, none of them is as good as the version printed in another collection. They do not have as much detail; two of the three are melodramatic and, since The Old Soak's view of history is not melodramatic, the stories do not fit into the book very comfortably. All three stories have familiar material which Marquis used on numerous occasions.[7]

Finally, Marquis's most profitable use of Clem Hawley was in *The Old Soak*, which ran for 423 performances on Broadway in 1922–1923, by far the longest run for any of his plays. It is an oldfashioned melodrama involving Clem Hawley, his family and friends. In his highly favorable review of *The Old Soak*, Alexander Woollcott dismissed the plot as unimportant, placing his emphasis on "the rich and abundant and delightful overlay of humor and whimsicality that makes the plot . . . a mere prop for a genuine and hearty entertainment . . . 'The Old Soak' is gorgeously entertaining . . . an authentic popular success."[8]

I would agree with Woollcott that the plot is insignificant, although it is successful as a parody of *The Drunkard* and other temperance melodramas. Basically, the drama revolves around the attempts of Cousin Webster Parsons, the village banker, to gain control of 100 shares of stock belonging to Clem's wife. Clem, Jr., or "Clemmie," Clem's weak-willed son, "borrows" the stock to repay money he has "borrowed" from his office in order to make an impression on Ina Heath, a "flapper" whom he has been courting. Clem takes the blame for the missing stock to spare his wife from finding out about Clemmie. Because of Matilda's anger over the missing stock, Clem leaves home to live at Jake Smith's hotel. After the stock gets into Cousin Webster's hands, Clem, as a true hero should do, resolves the situation. He goes to the bank and forces Cousin Webster to give back the $10,000 he has made from selling the stock by threatening to inform the police that Cousin Webster is a secret partner in Jake and Al's bootlegging operation. In the last scene of the play, Clem triumphantly gives his wife the $10,000. By now, Clemmie has confessed to his mother who, in typically melodramatic fashion, reveals her love for Clem and her belief in his basic goodness. Clem also reunited his daughter, Lucy, with her sweetheart, Tom. They had split over Lucy's defense of her father against all charges. The conclusion of *The Old Soak* is reminiscent of *The Bank Dick* and other W. C. Fields films where he triumphs at the end, even forcing his wife to accept his drinking. Generally, *The Old Soak* is similar to Joseph Jefferson's perennial classic, *Rip Van Winkle*, which, like *The Old Soak*, converts a basically comic work into a melodrama with comic scenes. In both plays, a seemingly lazy, irresponsible husband with a fondness for the bottle returns home to save his family and emerge as a hero.

Since the plot and characters are largely lifted from melodrama and other popular literature, what gives *The Old Soak* whatever distinctiveness it has? Chiefly, the character of Clem Hawley who is not much changed from the other works bearing his name. He is a lovable human being who likes to drink with his friends; he is not mean or nasty. Although much of the play is taken from Clem's earlier appearances in print, one of the most popular and most successful devices in the play is not in the other Hawley books. This is the introduction of Pete the Parrot, who is used to test the quality of Al's home brew. As reported by Nellie, the hired girl, a staunch ally of Clem's, the first trial brings about unexpected results:

HIRED GIRL. Oh, Mr. Hawley, Mr. Hawley, Mr. Hawley! I've thought for ten years that Peter was a gentleman parrot.
OLD SOAK. Ain't he? What's he done?
HIRED GIRL. I gave him two drinks of that hootch and—Mr. Hawley—he laid an egg!
OLD SOAK. (To PETER) Peter, you'll have to leave here if you can't hold your liquor like a man![9]

Later, in the most famous scene in the play, Peter dies:

AL. . . . What's the trouble with you, Nellie?
HIRED GIRL. (She eyes the bottle pointedly from time to time throughout the speech) It's Peter, that's the trouble. (Turns to Old Soak, begins to sniffle) Peter, he's gone, Mr. Hawley, he is. He's d-d-d-dead! Seriously dead! It happened a half hour ago. I think it was his constitution undermined itself with that hootch Al brought here the other night, and I never will forgive myself, I won't. But he kept coaxin' and coaxin' for it that pretty that I couldn't refuse him. "Salways fair weather, it is," he'd say, and then I'd give him a drink of it. And then he'd cock his head onto one side and say: "Nellie was a lady," thankin' me, he was. And he kept on drinking of it till he deceased himself with it. He called out to me about a half hour ago, he did. "Fair weather," he says, and then he laffed. Only he didn't laugh natural. Mr. Hawley, he laffed kind of puny and feeble like there was somethin' furrin weighin' onto his stomach. "I can't give you no more, Peter," I says to him, "for there ain't no more," I says. And then he streched his neck out and bit the wire on his cage and squawked, for he says in a kind of sad voice: "Nellie was a lady, she was," he says. And them was the last words he ever give utterings to Mr. Hawley.[10]

It is a scene like this or the scene in which Clem and Al pretend his living room is an old-time bar room that make the play entertaining today. Clem is given more dignity and heroic qualities in the play than he possesses in the books. Yet, this is not inconsistent with his role as a cracker barrel philosopherhero who stands behind such values as family, home, and Bible. In one exchange with Cousin Webster, early in the play, Clem clearly states his philosophy of life, a philosophy that would no doubt be shared by the vast majority of the audience:

OLD SOAK. I know your life. Everywhere you stepped there was a flower
withered up. You always been a spoil-sport and a kill-joy. . . ever since you
crawled out of your crib and traded a broken rattle for two good ones.
COUSIN WEBSTER. Kill-Joy? And you brought joy to your family, haven't
you?
OLD SOAK. No. I been a failure; I couldn't see nothin' but joy in the world
and I run after it too hard and quick and never done much else. But just the
same, I always knowed it was the only real thing. And you never knowed it
was there at all. When you guessed at it, you hated it.[11]

The sequel to *The Old Soak, Everything's Jake*, opened on June 16,
1930. It did not recapture the popularity of the original, running for
seventy-six performances. In this play, Marquis uses, loosely, the format of *The Old Soak's History of the World*, putting Clem, Al, and
Jake in Europe (Anthony, 488). Marquis also developed the part of
"Hennery" Withers, the "damn little athyiss" so disliked by The Old
Soak, into a man with an obsession to place a wreath on Voltaire's tomb
(Anthony, 489). He was quite disappointed when the play did not have
the success of *The Old Soak*, but, as he admitted, "a sequel is an
admission that you've been reduced to imitating yourself" (Anthony,
487).

On the whole, Clem Hawley was very profitable for Don Marquis.
Today, since Prohibition is no longer an issue, The Old Soak does not
have the comic appeal he offered in the 1920s. However, as a common-
sense cracker-barrel "wise fool," he is in the direct line of native American humor, representing a conservative, humane view of human
nature. Like other American sages, Clem Hawley knows that people
are not basically very good, but he also knows that they must be loved
as they are if life is to have any meaning.[12]

II   *Hermione and Her Little Group of Serious Thinkers*

Besides The Old Soak, one of the earliest humorous characters created by Marquis in "The Sun Dial" was Hermione, the wealthy dilet-
tante. In 1916, he published *Hermione and Her Little Group of Serious Thinkers* (hereafter called *Hermione*), drawn from the column.
The character of Hermione grew out of Marquis's intense dislike of
pretension.

Marquis introduced Hermione in "The Sun Dial" after a visit he and

Reina made to Greenwich Village. The opening "Proem" in *Hermione*
reflects his first impression of Bohemia:

> . . .
> There, there, they sit and cerebrate:
> The fervid Poete who never potes,
> Great Artists, Male or She, that Talk
> But scorn the Pigment and the Chalk,
> And Cubist sculptors, wild as Goats.
> Theosopists and Swamis, too,
> Musicians made as Hatters be-
> (E'en puzzled Hatters, two or three!)
> Tame Anarchists, a dreary crew,
> Squib Socialists too damp to sosh
> Fake Hobohemians steeped in suds,
> Glib Females in Artistic Duds
> With Captive Husbands cowed and gauche.[13]

As the "Proem" shows, the tone of *Hermione* is not a bitter one.
Anthony states that this book shows Marquis " . . . at his best as a deadpan comic" (Anthony, 171). What he apparently means is that Marquis
allows Hermione and her group to speak for themselves without showing his own distaste very much.

When published, *Hermione* got generally good reviews; one
reviewer saw Hermione's monologues " . . . as a sort of satirical ency-
clopedia of the literary, artistic, and philosophical fads that infest
America at the present day."[14] The same reviewer compares Marquis
with Molière, specifically seeing each writer making fun of young
ladies and their salons. Another critic thought Hermione was as vital
as Mr. Dooley which was high praise indeed considering Dooley's
immense popularity in early twentieth century America.[15]

More recent critics have also treated *Hermione* kindly. Bernard
DeVoto insisted in 1950 that " . . . Hermione is with us still, and Fothergil Finch, and her whole group. Their stuff is in a different key from
the original one; but only the key ever changes, the melody is the same
forever. . . ."[16] A later critic calls Hermione Marquis's "liveliest work"
after *Archy and Mehitabel,* seeing Hermione as a "lady" who pretends
to be daring as a contrast to Mehitabel who is daring but pretends to
be a lady.[17] A more recent critic calls Hermione, Marquis's " . . . richest
satirical creation," insisting that she applies equally will to the present:
"Ought not Hermione to be required reading for all superficial young

intellectuals who believe that history began only when they became aware of it?"[18]

Like *The Old Soak, Hermione* is a collection of columns, almost all of them monologues by Hermione. Once one gets past the introductory poem, the book is not organized in any particular order. Hermione is pathetically shallow and self-centered. Yet, Marquis does not treat her savagely, in the grand manner of classic satire. He is aiming at those who pretend to be intellectuals, who pretend to be artists, who pretend to be concerned, but who flit from fad to fad without ever going beneath the surface where they might actually have to do something or produce a real work of art.

Hermione would consider her monologues as works of art. She delivers each one very seriously:

> I'm taking up Bergson this week.
>   Next week I'm going to take up Etruscan
>   vases and the Montessori system.
> Oh, no, I haven't lost my interest in sociology.
> Only the other night we went down in the auto
> and watched the breadline. (*Hermione*, 59)

This is a typical Hermione chain of thought. Each week, or possibly each day, there will be something new to "take up." Yet, it is always "taken up" from the viewpoint of the idle rich, who can afford to patronize anyone or anything offering a relief from boredom. Of course, Hermione is "sincere" in her interest in sociology, seeing no conflict in watching the bread line from an automobile. While watching, she thinks of how the world is getting better; people are willing to make sacrifices for others. "Not that I was really so uncomfortable in the auto, you know, I had on my new mink coat . . ." (*Hermione*, 61).

Hermione's continual frustration at not being appreciated by the working class doesn't stop her from planning for its betterment. While uncertain as to how to handle the effects of drinking on the working class, she is prepared to impose Spartan-like measures: "But the working classes must be saved from themselves, even if all the employers of labor have to write out a list of just what they shall eat and drink and make them buy only those things" (*Hermione*, 152). In this situation, as in many others, she relies on her father's checkbook to support her latest cause: "So I coaxed another check out of Papa to help destroy Capitalism and Parasites."[19] Her father has only scorn for her friends and fads, but, as a typical comic father, comes through with the money. What other function could he have? Of course, Hermione sees no conflict in taking money from "Papa" to fight capitalism, reform the parasite woman, or support some new artist she has discovered.

Besides her concern for the working class, Hermione is anxious to help other oppressed groups. She is interested in prison reform, announcing she is ready to do anything to help the convicts:

Collect Money . . . or give talks, or read books about them, or make any other sacrifice.

Even get them jobs . . . though as far as hiring one of them myself, or rather getting Papa to—well, really, you know, one must draw the line somewhere. (*Hermione*, 139)

Again, Marquis is taking a shot at those who are willing to talk about reform, but are not willing to personally become involved, giving themselves instead of merely their money or thoughts.

When World War I reaches her little group, she is rather upset because her mother doesn't realize that the Belgians are going out and the Poles are coming in. In keeping with her character, Hermione is optimistic about the war, believing it will not affect her country or the things she values most. There are no beautiful old things in America that could be bombarded in a war; besides, if the United States went to war " . . . someone like Edison would invent something quick, you know, and it would be all over in a few hours" (*Hermione*, 57).

When Hermione takes up a fad, she does not stay with it any longer than she does with a cause, moving from dew hopping to twilight sleep to the Swami Brandranath. She is impressed by the Swami's silk robes, by the "pure" look in his eyes. In fact she finds that all things Oriental are wonderful: "And just think of India with all its yogis and bazaars and mahatmas and rajahs and things" (*Hermione*, 23). When the Swami explains about caste marks and one of the Serious Thinkers asks him if he is tattooed, Hermione is properly indignant. Later, when it is revealed that the Swami has been married seven times, Hermione has a properly spiritual explanation: "But he wasn't really a bigamist at all. You see, he had seven spiritual planes . . . he could get from one plane to another quite easily" (*Hermione*, 30).

Hermione's defense of the Swami, her interest in the *Bhagavad Gita*, her love of anything Far Eastern are vulgarized reflections of the

genuine interest in the Orient and the exotic which was highly pronounced in early twentieth-century America. Undoubtedly, Marquis
uses Hermione to support his suspicion of the American tendency to
praise something because it is new or exotic and to deal with this new
fad superficially.

The fad that Marquis disliked as strongly as any was the one with
which Hermione became most closely involved—vers libre. In the
years immediately before World War I, vers libre was an emotional
issue, with the Imagists—Amy Lowell, Ezra Pound, and their support-
ers—hurling charges and countercharges at one another. In *Archy and
Mehitabel,* Marquis makes his dislike of vers libre quite clear. In *Hermione,* largely through the character of Fothergil Finch, Marquis
attacks the image of the vers libre bard; to Marquis, saying someone is
a vers libre bard is simply another way of saying one is a fake.

Fothergil Finch (the name in itself is comic as is "Hermione") is
Hermione's ideal artist; he has spiritual, not physical, virility. Before
any examples of his art have been given, Fothergil is scorned as physically weak and lazy. His continual concern with virility, with his being
a virile vers libre bard, suggests homosexual traits. The closest Hermione comes to implying this is in commenting on a vers libre poem
about strength and virility, written by Fothergil: "Fothergil is just simply fascinated by strength and virility, though you would never think
it to look at him . . . you'd think . . . that he'd be writing about violets
instead of cave men" (*Hermione,* 142).

Fothergil, of course, sees himself as an "artist" in revolt against
society; he invites, even welcomes, persecution:

> You ask me, do you, what I am in revolt against?
> Against you, fool, dolt, idiot, against you, against everything!
> Against Heaven, Hell, and punctuation . . . against Life,
>   Death, rhyme and rhythm . . .
> Persecute me, now, persecute me, curse you, persecute me!
> Slave that you are . . . what do Marriage, Toothbrushes,
>   Nail-files, the Decalogue, Handkerchiefs, Newton's
>   Law of Gravity, Capital, Barbers, Property, Publishers,
>   Courts, Rhyming Dictionaries, Clothes, Dollars, mean
>   to Me?
> I am a Giant, I am a Titan, I am a Hercules of Liberty, I
>   am Prometheus, I am the Jess Willard of the New
>   Cerebral Pugilism, I am the Modern Cave Man, I am

the Comrade of the Cosmic Urge, I have kicked off the
Boots of Superstition, and I run wild along the Milky
Way without ingrowing toenails.
I am I!
Curse you, what are You?
You are only You!
Nothing more!
Ha!
Ba . . . persecute me, now persecute me! (*Hermione*, 25–26)

This combination of self-pity, formlessness, and scrambled images
makes vers libre ridiculous. It also makes vers libre seem very easy to
write. In fact, Hermione becomes a vers libre poet, although she
believes "if I lived a hundred years I never could make two lines
rhyme with each other" (*Hermione*, 63). Fothergil believes rhyme is
out of fashion, so Hermione "just dashed" off a vers libre poem. In one
night, she writes twenty or thirty poems, allowing the reader to share
three of them:

What becomes of
People when they die?
I used to ask when I was a little child,
And now even since
I am grown up I am not sure that I know.

I see the rain fall.
It is no effort for the rain to fall.
Why is it no effort?
Because it falls spontaneously!

O Spontaneity! Spontaneity!
Rain is genius,
Genius is rain!
Fall, fall, rain.

I see the moon out of the window.
I wonder what it thinks of me?
Wouldn't the moon and I both be surprised
If we found out that neither one of us
Thought anything at all about the other? (*Hermione*, 63–65)

Marquis is obviously satirizing the ease with which vers libre can be dashed off. The extreme shallowness of the verse is a strong criticism of vers libre.

As usual, Hermione sees her poetic success as another way to dramatize herself:

Fothy is going to get them published . . . if Papa will put up the money, and one nice thing about poor dear Papa is that he will always put it up. . . . The book's going to be in vellum, you know, and that sort of thing. I'm going to have a gown just like the cover and give a fete when it comes out. (*Hermione*, 64–65)

Fothergil Finch combines the shallowness, pretentiousness, posturing, and the false virility and strength Marquis associated with Greenwich Village and, on a broader level, bad art in general. As a modern poet, Fothergil finds beauty and poetic subjects in unlikely places. He has written a series of poems on the beauty of mud, sneezes, the influenza germ, hiccoughs, bugs, the dogfish, a glue factory, a buzzard, and a hyena in a zoo. He is especially taken with garbage scows because their spiritual significance will never be understood by the bourgeois. On leaving the opening of Hermione's salon, Marquis asks a garbage man about garbage scows. The garbage man replies that nearly everything in life comes his way and gets dumped in the bay. This inspires Marquis to write a more conventional poem about garbage scows:

> Symbolic Garbage Man! *Sans* rest or pause,
> In steadfast faith work for thy sacred Cause!
> Some time, perhaps, all piles of twisted bunk,
> All half-baked faddists, heaps of mental junk,
> Unto the waiting Scow we'll cart away
> Eventual to dump 'em down the bay! (*Hermione*, 108)

This is what he believes will happen to Hermione, to Fothergil, and to other members of her group. However, the final "Envoy," called "Hermione, the Deathless," makes it clear that while Hermione, as an individual, will fall victim to the garbage man, her type will continue:

> She will not die!—in Brainstorm Slum
>   Fake, Nut and Freak Psychologist
> Eternally shall buzz and hum,

> And Spook and Swami keep their tryst
> With Thinkers in a Mental Mist.
> You threaten her with Night and
>   Sorrow?
> Out of the silences, I wist,
>
> More Little Groups will rise tomorrow!
> (*Hermione*, 187)

If Marquis were alive today, he would certainly find Hermione alive and well everywhere, possibly a little more worldly, but still in the grip of each new fad.

CHAPTER 5

Marquis as Poet: "Cursed with an Incorrigible Mirth"

ALMOST everyone who writes about Don Marquis agrees that above all else Marquis is a poet and, at his best, a comic poet.[1] However, there is less agreement about the quality of his nonhumorous poetry. If Marquis's best poetry were to be selected for a one-volume publication, almost all the poems selected would be comic.

I Problems of a Comic Poet

Overall, comic verse itself is not that critically well received. "There is no denying the fact that verse written solely to amuse is at a disadvantage on the critical scale. Perhaps because it lays no serious claim to distinction it is not presumed to be distinguished."[2] Possibly, critics have found comic verse difficult to take seriously because it isn't poetic in the traditional sense. It is not didactic, and it doesn't make "poetic" statements about love, nature, or country. Whether or not much of Marquis's comic verse is " . . . superior in technique, freshness and subtlety to many first rate lyrics,"[3] at its best, it is an art.

Marquis's own view of the comic poet is stated in two poems, both titled "The Jesters." The first of the two is a lament to fools who perish without leaving a sign, who, throughout history, have mocked wise men, men of affairs, but who, for all that, may have more clearly sensed the meaning of life than those they mock.[4]

The second "Jesters" is a more ambitious poem in which Marquis speaks for the jesters throughout history who have been " . . . cursed with an incorrigible mirth."[5]

> Still, when we reach the dark way's darkest end
> And by the blind wall droop with none to friend,
> Then, of a sudden,

Some perverse humour shakes us, and we laugh!
Some tricky thought will grip us, and we laugh!
Some rebel mood will seize us and we laugh![6]

Such irreverence deserves punishment from the gods,

        . . .but in the end
                  some brother
    clown
With desperate mirth will laugh your foolish godhead down![7]

    The "curse" of laughter cannot be denied. Although its possessor
may not be happy, he will have power to mock humanity. The jester
is cut off from society because of his laughter at the wrong moments,
because of his inability to show respect whether the respect is deserved
or not. In "The Tavern of Despair," Marquis takes a much more negative view of the comic poet. The inhabitants of the tavern are "was-
trels" and "fools" who have destroyed whatever talents they had:

Not one of us but had some pearls
    And flung them to the swine,
Not one of us but had some gift—
    Some spark of fire divine—
Each might have been God's minister
    In the temple of some art—
Each feels his gift perverted move
    Wormlike through his dry heart.[8]

Marquis sees the fools-jesters mocking what they love for the sake of
paradox. Whatever genuine talent they have has been thrown away.
Throwing away such a gift as poetry offends the gods. Thus, Marquis
certainly would despair at being acclaimed largely a comic poet, even
though he was much better at this type of poem.

II   *The Comic Poetry*

    As a good comic poet, Marquis takes none of the great poetic sub-
jects, such as love and death, very seriously. On a superficial level, his
series of "Improbable Epitaphs" make fun of a poetic convention that

had been fair game for other American humorists. An example of this series is the epitaph for Solomon Gay:

> A REMARKABLE MAN
> WAS SOLOMON GAY
> WHO IS PLANTED
>   HERE
> TILL THE JUDGMENT DAY.
>   WHEN HE FOUND
>   HE HAD NOTHING
>   IMPORTANT TO SAY
>   HE WOULD KEEP HIS MOUTH
>   SHUT
>   AND GO ON HIS WAY.[9]

   Another Marquis poem, with a more complex view of death, is "Proverbs xii, 7." The Bible verse reads, "The wicked are overthrown and are no more, but the house of the righteous will stand." Marquis's sonnet interprets this verse from the viewpoint of the gunmen and gangsters of the 1920s, using slang with considerable effectiveness:

> Fate is the Gunman that all gunmen dread;
> Fate stings the Stinger for his roll of green;
> Fate, strong-arm Worker, on the bean
> Of strong-arm workers bumps his pipe of lead.
>
> Oh, cross guy, Fate is cross—a super crook
> That stands in with the dicks to get you jugged;
> Fate has you measured, numbered, tagged and mugged,
> And keeps your thumb prints in a little book!
>
> Take it from David's son, the thought profound:
> The Gonoph's due to go away from here!
> Where are the busy mobs of yesteryear?—
> Somehow we do not find them sticking round!
>
> Some lammistered to get a change of air.
> Some are in Stir. And some sat in the Chair.[10]

By using Fate as a gunman, the master con artist who "stings" all others and a "super crook" who is also in league with the law, Marquis builds up a highly comic effect. The last two stanzas make the poem even more comic. The parody of Villon's poem "Ballade of Dead Ladies" in the third line of the third stanza is properly unromantic about crime. The closing couplet with three unpleasant possibilities ends the sonnet on a rather grim note, although the light tone of the whole poem makes the conclusion less grim than might be expected. Marquis does not worry about supporting the original verse from Proverbs, but he is concerned with using the sonnet form to reflect, not very seriously, on the inevitability of Fate.

Marquis's fondness for the sonnet led him to write three sonnet sequences: "Sonnets to a Red-Haired Lady," "Savage Portraits," and "Love Sonnets of a Caveman." The first sequence consists of thirty-five sonnets, largely dealing with the imaginary sonneteer's many marriages, all to redheads who met violent ends:

> Old Titian loved your sort of fiery mop,
> And down his leagues of canvas, crowned with flame,
> Walks one long pageant of Torchlight Dames,
> Nor hath Oblivion any traffic cop
> To bid that bright procession swerve or stop . . .
> I've heard your brother call you Burning Shame:
> Some day I'll bend that poor simp's vital frame
> Beyond repair! Suzanne, sweet Carrot Top,
>
> When we are wedded, prithee, don't allow
> Your idiot relations near our house . . .
> My Third Wife's father wagged a silly pow
> In all our councils, Susan. Welladay!
> They lie in one grave now, my erstwhile spouse,
> And he, her sire, who gave the bride away.[11]

In III (quoted above) the sonneteer mixes Titian's fondness for red-haired women with the contrasting image of a traffic cop and a red light—creating an irreverent tone. He than shifts to a threat toward Suzanne's brother, closing the octave with a "sentimental" reference to his wife-to-be. The sestet is more negative, although still basically humorous. The closing lines of the sonnet, with the abrupt announcement of the double grave, contrast with "Welladay," which is used throughout the sequence to add a comic fatalism and a tone of resignation.

Throughout this sonnet sequence, there is a great deal of violence:

One wife is choked; one is killed by driving hairpins into her head; one is poisoned along with her father; another is scalped. In all these cases, the wife's demise is brought about by her bad habits, her interference with her husband's life, or her refusal to disavow her family. The humor in the sonnets comes from the rather idealized treatment of the poet's current wife or fiancee in the early part of the sonnet and the violence contained in the sestet. Violence, hostility toward in-laws, and dislike of any threat to one's individuality may still be found in a good deal of contemporary humor.

Marquis's second sonnet sequence, "Savage Portraits," is a series of thirty-four sonnets, each depicting a human type Marquis particularly disliked—hypocrites, false wits, misers, and snobs. Each sonnet bears the name of the person described in the sonnet, with the name often suggesting the subject: "Boond" is a money king who has no soul; "Dirk" is a supposed wit; "Browber" is a wife beater. By treating these people objectively and letting their actions speak for themselves, Marquis creates a bitter, humorous tone. The sonnets are not all savage, and, at times, Marquis overpowers the subject. Yet, on the whole, he does attain a fine blend of indignation and humor in such sonnets as "Phyllida":

> Phyllida's young—but skilled in self-control;
> Phyllida's fair—of that Phyllida's sure;
> Phyllida's pure—notoriously pure;
> Phyllida's wise—when snaring men's her goal;
> Phyllida's innocent—when that's her role;
> With deft and silken craft, occult, obscure,
> She makes her proven purity a lure;
> Phyllida's virtuous, in all but soul!
>
> Phyllida's always outraged when she's played
> The very hell Phyllida planned to play.
> I spoke the latest fool Phyllida's made:
> "Were this," he mused, "a franker, elder day,
> Long since some amorous dagger had caressed
> The lovely hollow of Phyllida's breast!"[12]

Here, Marquis uses the image of the femme fatale, hardly a comic figure, but the use of contrast in each line of the octave is what makes the sonnet humorous and effective. The suggestion that Phyllida is morally, if not physically, corrupt makes her more complex.

On a less bitter level, Marquis succeeds quite well, in the vein of E. A. Robinson's "Miniver Cheevy," in his portrait of "Pedder":

> If this base country had not cast off kings,
> So Pedder's manner hints, he'd be an earl . . .
> He talks of "Demos" and his thin lips curl . . .
> A rumpled grace that speaks of courtlier things,
> So Pedder fancies, round about him clings . . .
> The swine of trade will never trade this pearl;
> He does not toil; from churl to common churl
> He makes his way with lordly borrowings.
>
> His overcoat he flings on like a cloak,
> He writes romantic verses . . . with a quill . . .
> Once, when some ribald fellow dared to joke
> Of the late Queen Bess he sobbed and cried, "Be still!"
> Another time, caught drunk and unaware,
> He showed me how one works a barber's chair.[13]

Pedder is a snob who refuses to lower himself to battling for success. However, he cannot survive without "lordly borrowings," just as Miniver Cheevy must have the gold he scorns. The references to writing verse with a quill and particularly the reference to the "late" Queen Bess, who, apparently, has been dead for only a few years, make Pedder ridiculous without making him unlikable. Finally, the concluding couplet raises the question of whether or not Pedder has been a barber and whether he must be drunk to accept reality.

The third sonnet sequence, "Love Sonnets of a Cave Man," mixes violence and passion, as in "Sonnets to a Red-Haired Lady." The eleventh sonnet, "An Ancient Souvenir," does this quite well:

> I loitered through a museum and there
> I saw, new-hinged with wire, tricked out for show,
> The skull I had a million years ago;
> The lipless thing grinned with a knowing air,
> The eyeless sockets gave me stare for stare,
> And oh, my Sweet! the crown still holds the dent
> You made that memorable morn you bent
> The grid on it and left it grilled and bare.
> How fashions change in skulls! We wore them thick
> And sloping quickly backward from the eyes

> When I was in my primal lustihood;
> And did a lover bounce a playful brick
> Upon her lover's sconce it was but food
> For happy laughter, then. Ah me! Time flies![14]

In this sonnet there is a nostalgic longing for the good old days when passion could be fully expressed, when conscience or the moral sense were not important. By connecting a childlike innocence with violence, Marquis creates a comic tone that he sustains throughout much of the sequence. Clearly, the sonnet was a form Marquis enjoyed and was able to use humorously with considerable skill.

In his humorous poetry, as in his humorous prose, Marquis refused to be awed by the past. "Famous Love Affairs" gives a generally satirical treatment of romance throughout history, beginning with Adam and Eve. In Marquis's treatment of the fall, Satan is " . . . a City man," who, as the conventional melodramatic villain, takes revenge on two innocents by posing as their friend. The conclusion makes God into an angry landlord who doesn't appreciate leasebreakers:

> He rooned em . . . then he gave a
>   hiss,
> a glide and boa-constricted . . .
> Details are told in Genesis . . .
> I think they were evicted.[15]

Another poem in the series, "Petrarch and Laura," ridicules the sonneteer who dedicated his life to creating beautiful poetry about a woman he would never love sexually:

> She loved her husband. And her home.
> She loved her Babes. She had eleven.
> While Petrarch wrote pome after pome—
> Sonnets three-hundred-twenty-seven.[16]

Predictably, in his comic poetry Marquis did not treat the present any more reverently than the past. As in his prose humor, he made fun of Prohibition, particularly in his versions of the temperance ballad. "Down in a Wine Vault" deals with Nanny, an "angel-child" coming to her grandfather who is drinking booze in a wine vault with an aged

comrade. Unlike the temperance ballad, her pleading has an unfore-
seen ending:

> In came a little Tot for to kiss her granny,
>   Such a little totty she could scarcely tottle,
> Saying, "Kiss me, Grandpa! Kiss your little Nanny!"
>   But the old man beaned her with a whiskey bottle![17]

Grandpa's companion criticizes him for striking hasty. The reply
would gladden W. C. Fields's heart:

> All around the world little tots are begging
>   Grandpas and daddies for to quit their lushing.
> Reformers eggs 'em on. I am tired of egging!
>   Tired of being cowed, cowering and blushing!
>
> I struck for freedom! I'm a man of mettle!
>   Though I never would 'a' done it had I not been drinking—
> From Athabasca south to Popocatepetl
>   We must strike for freedom, quit our shirking![18]

The appeal to freedom gives the poem mock-heroic overtones. Then,
in the last stanza, after the two old men have agreed that Nanny got
what she deserved, Marquis throws in a properly indignant moral
which should satisfy the Prohibitionists:

> Down in a wine vault underneath the city
>   They sat drinking while the snow was falling.
> Wicked old men with scarcely any pity—
>   The moral of my tale is quite appalling![19]

The ballad is almost a reversal of the famous "Father, Dear Father,
Come Home with Me Now" from *Ten Nights in a Bar-Room*. In the
play, Little Mary Morgan's death turns her father into a reformed
drunkard who spearheads the temperance movement in his village. In
his version, Marquis succeeds because he is content to use the form to
satirize itself without trying for great depth.

Marquis's own favorite among his comic poems was "Noah an'
Jonah an' Cap'n John Smith." The poem, which is set in Heaven and
revolves around an exchange of stories among these three famous
adventurers, was frequently reprinted in his column and in various

books. During the course of the poem, each of the three brags about his greatest feat. Noah claims to have provided for the entire Ark:

> Often I have ketched in a single hour on Monday
> Sharks enough to feed the fambly till Sunday—
> To feed all the sarpints, the tigers an' donkeys,
> To feed all the zebras, the insects an' monkeys,
> . . .
> To feed all the oxen, feed all the asses,
> Feed all the bisons an' little hoppergrasses—
> Always I ketched, in half a hour on Monday,
> All that the fambly could gormandize till Sunday![20]

Cap'n John Smith admits to having fought and defeated wild men and wild beasts, but his greatest challenge was in fighting octopuses:

> I'd rub my forehead with phosphorescent light
> An' plunge into the ocean an' seek 'em out at night!
> . . .
> When they seen the bright light blazin' on my forehead
> They used to rush at me, screaming something horrid!
> Tentacles wavin', teeth white an' gnashin',
> Hollerin' an' bellerin', wallerin' an' splashin'!
> I useter grab 'em as they rushed from their grots,
> Ketch all their legs an' tie 'em into knots![21]

Jonah is not impressed with either of the two fishermen:

> You think yer fishermen! You think yer great!
> All I asks is this: Has one of ye been *bait?*
> Cap'n Noah, Cap'n John, I heerd when ye hollered;
> What I asks is this: Has one of ye been *swallered?*
> . . .
> When I seen the strong fish, wallopin' like a lummicks,
> I useter foller 'em, dive into their stummicks!
> I could v'yage an' steer 'em, I could understand 'em,
> I useter navigate 'em, I useter land 'em!
> Don't you pester *me* with any more narration!
> Go git famous! Git a reputation![22]

The humor comes from the use of dialect which doesn't seem quite fitting for three such famous figures, especially in heaven. The poem uses the very American device of the tall tale, but also has a relaxed,

idyllic tone, presenting an eternity that these three deserve and one
that all men should yearn for—an eternity where one may tell stories
and enjoy life; in other words the final realization of Marquis's Almost
Perfect State.

In his comic poetry, Marquis does not use any new techniques. He
is content to use established forms such as the sonnet or ballad. His
humor comes from the irreverent treatment of "poetic" subjects such
as love, death, and motherhood. Obviously, much of his comic verse is
superficial and will not offer much beyond the surface. However, in
his sonnets in particular, Marquis must certainly be ranked in the top
level of American comic poets.

III   *The Noncomic Poetry*

After reading Marquis's nonhumorous poems, one wants to reread
only a few of them. Marquis does take a conventional view of most
subjects; however, when dealing with his ever-beloved "cosmic" questions, he could rise to the occasion. In his first published volume of
poetry, he states his attitude, which he maintained throughout his life,
toward the concept of a god. As the title suggests, "The God-Maker
Man" sees the gods as having been created by man's need for a god or
gods:

As the forehead of Man grows broader, so do his creeds;
And his gods they are shaped in his image and mirror his needs;
And he clothes them with thunder and beauty, he clothes them with music
    and fire;
Seeing not, as he bows by their altars, that he worships his own desire;
And mixed with his trust there is terror, and mixed with his madness is
    ruth,
And every man grovels in error, yet every man glimpses a truth.[23]

Marquis believes that all gods created by man's expanding need for a
deity are worthy, but that no one of them is the ultimate deity! His
description of how man creates his gods is vivid without being too sim-
plistic. However, it is not often that he can sustain this sort of effect. In
addition, it is not at all certain that the use of rather obvious rhymed
lines in this poem adds at all to the effectiveness.

At times, when dealing with less "cosmic" subjects, Marquis is more
successful as a nonhumorous poet. "New York" (1925) is his attempt to
deal with the spirit of that city as Sandburg had dealt with Chicago in

his famous poem, published in 1916. Most readers of both poems would agree that Sandburg is much more effective. He does not use conventional forms in dealing with a contemporary subject, whereas Marquis relies largely on conventional rhyme and meter. Similar to Sandburg's view of Chicago, Marquis does see New York as both beautiful and ugly:

> I have spun with her dervish priests;
> I have searched to the souls of her hunted beasts
> And found love sleeping there;
> I have soared on the wings of her flashing dreams;
> I have sunk with her dull despair;
> I have sweat with her travails and cursed with her pains;
> I have swelled with her foolish pride;
> I have raged through a thick red mist at one with her
>   branded Cains,
> With her broken Christs have died.[24]

"Branded Cains" and "broken Christs" do not have the power of Sandburg's hog butchers and painted women. In all fairness, Sandburg and Marquis are writing about two different cities; Chicago is young and virile; New York is older and more decadent. Yet, the fact remains that Sandburg defined Chicago for many people, but no one would think automatically of Marquis's poem when New York is mentioned.

In the introductory "Proem" to his first published book of poetry, Marquis takes a rather resigned view of his poetry, passing it off as not being what he intended it to be:

> So let them pass, these songs of mine,
> Into oblivion, nor repine;
> Abandoned ruins of larger schemes,
> Dimmed lights adrift from noblier dreams. . . .[25]

Later, in the same poem, he states that love, laughter, and fighting are the supreme human values. Certainly, this reflects the young Marquis's attitude—an attitude that finds its supreme expression in *Archy and Mehitabel*. As Marquis grew older, he grew more capable of looking at himself critically, seeing how far he had strayed from this romantic view. In fact, when Marquis looked at himself carefully, he could produce poetry of a rather high quality. "A Gentleman of Fifty Soliloquizes" moves between seriousness and humor. Basically the poem deals with the compromises a man makes with life by the time he reaches middle age. After a first stanza in which he presents the dilemma of being false to ourselves in order to be true to friends, Marquis becomes both more pessimistic and more humorous:

> The valour cold to be ourselves we lack;
>   And so from strands of kindness misconstrued
> And lenient moments, careless threads and slack
>   We're meshed within a web of habitude.
>
> And often these are worthier men than we;
>   But that itself, in time, becomes offense;
> We're burdened with this damned nobility
>   That's forced upon us, which we must recompense.
>
> We loath ourselves for being insincere,
>   And lavish generous deeds to hide the fact:
> For who could wound these hearts? Thus we appear
>   Thrice loyal friends in word and look and act!
>
> And golden lies with which we save them pain
> But serve to make their true regard more fain.[26]

By being kind instead of being ourselves, we weaken ourselves as individuals, giving in to " . . . this damned nobility." Marquis is still given to the conventionally poetic word, such as "fain," but he is more successful here in dealing with human nature than in dealing with "cosmic" questions.

As a nonhumorous poet, Marquis is seldom, if ever, first-rate. He relies too easily on conventional subjects, forms, and images without making them very interesting or very provocative. Certainly, one can find some readable, competent poems among Marquis's nonhumorous poetry. However, if Marquis is remembered for poetry other than *Archy and Mehitabel*, it will be for his comic sonnets and burlesques; in these, he was able to use his imagination and talents most effectively.

CHAPTER 6

Marquis as Novelist

ALTHOUGH Don Marquis was known primarily as a columnist and as the author of short humorous sketches and poems, his first published book, *Danny's Own Story*, 1912, was a novel. Between the publication of *Danny's Own Story* and Marquis's death in 1937, he published two other novels. In 1939, after his death, *Sons of the Puritans*, his uncompleted novel, was published.

Marquis's friends and contemporary critics were much more drawn to his poetry and short humor than to his novels. Except for Christopher Morley, who regarded Marquis as a great American writer, one finds few references to his novels among articles written about him during his lifetime. The bulk of his fiction is not memorable. Like Twain and other American humorists, Marquis did not write so well when confined to an established genre. Marquis, like Twain, was a natural storyteller; however, his four novels, one uncompleted at his death, are entertaining works which fall well short of being distinguished.

I Danny's Own Story

Although *Danny's Own Story* was not published until January 1912, Marquis had been thinking about the novel while he was working in Atlanta. His wife persuaded him to finish it in the summer of 1911. Two things should be noticed about the novel's gestation and birth. First, Marquis produced several synopses of the novel before settling on one he thought would work well. Second, the novel was accepted by the first publisher to whom Marquis sent it, Doubleday, Page and Company. This fits with the general pattern of Marquis's career in that he had little difficulty marketing his work. *Danny's Own Story* was well received, giving Marquis considerable recognition.

When one reads *Danny's Own Story* today, it is clear that, as most critics have stated, it was heavily influenced by Twain, particularly by

Huck Finn. In fact, *Danny's Own Story* was illustrated by E. W. Kemble, who had illustrated *Huck Finn* almost thirty years earlier. Another influence, less noted, is the heavy reliance on melodrama which weakens the novel's effectiveness although it may well have contributed to its original popularity.

The novel, told in the first person by Danny, begins with his description of how he was found on Hank Walters's doorstep in a basket. Hank and Elmira, his wife, raise Danny although there is no love between Hank and Danny. When he is eighteen, Danny fights with Hank and runs away with Dr. Kirby, who is operating an Indian medicine show. The rest of the novel deals with Danny's wanderings, with and without Doc Kirby, throughout the Midwest and the South. He gets involved with night riders in Kentucky and a lynching in Georgia where he and Doc Kirby are trying to sell a medicine that will turn Negroes white. At the conclusion of the novel, Danny discovers that Doc Kirby is his real father; this ties together Danny's wanderings and a rather melodramatic subplot involving a Miss Hampton, who is really Lucy Buckner, Danny's mother. She had run off to marry Doc Kirby, then left him and gone to Galesburg, Illinois, to have his child. Her brother had left Danny on Hank's doorstep. The two plots are connected when the medicine show plays Miss Hampton's town and Danny falls in love with her ward, Martha, who tells him how unhappy Miss Hampton is. However, it is not until the last chapter of the novel that the two plots are totally connected.

Obviously, whatever interest *Danny's Own Story* has for today's reader does not come from the plot. It is too melodramatic and too neatly resolved. Try to imagine *Huck Finn* ending with the revelation that Miss Watson or the Widow Douglas was really Huck's mother, or that he and Tom Sawyer had the same father! The plot of Marquis's first novel could almost be seen as a parody of melodrama; however, it is doubtful if that is what he had in mind. As anyone who reads much of Marquis's work will soon realize, he has a sentimental, romantic view of life that, in his best work, is under control, but is usually present to some degree.

Another problem with the novel is the lack of credibility of narrator and main character, Danny. Marquis makes it clear that, at the time Danny runs off with Doc Kirby, Danny is eighteen. Yet, throughout the novel, Danny often acts more like thirteen or fourteen. He seems almost totally unaware of how to associate with the opposite sex and is very naive in general. Granted, he is illiterate and has spent his life in a totally provincial environment. Nevertheless, if Marquis had lowered his age by three or four years, his narrative would be more convincing.

With these weaknesses, what makes the novel of any interest to a present-day reader? First, it is entertaining. A number of individual episodes are well done, particularly a scene at the beginning of the novel where Hank falls in a cistern while drunk. Believing that Hank has drowned, Danny reports his death to the town, only to discover that Hank is still alive. At this point, Hank's wife and Brother Cartwright, a Baptist preacher, refuse to let Hank out of the well until he signs the pledge. Finally, after being in the cistern for hours, Hank agrees to sign the pledge; it is lowered to him on a Bible and, when he makes his mark, Brother Cartwright leans into the cistern and baptizes him into the church. Hank then accuses Brother Cartwright of playing a dirty trick on him. Other people in the town agree, with the result that Brother Cartwright loses his job and Hank becomes even meaner to Danny than before he fell into the cistern. Marquis was so fond of this particular story that he reprinted it in *The Revolt of the Oyster* in a slightly condensed version and then used the same plot for stories in *The Old Soak's History of the World* and *Sons of the Puritans*.

Like *Huck Finn*, *Danny's Own Story* is interesting because it takes a naive narrator and allows him to tell of his adventures while wandering through a rather large area of the United States. Marquis handles the vernacular fairly well here. Danny's speech is believable much of the time. For instance, Danny describes Hank's use of profanity while he is trapped in the cistern:

He busted his own records and riz higher'n his own water marks for previous times. . . . They was deep down curses, that come from the heart. . . . It busted out every few minutes . . . and it was personal too. Hank, he would listen until he hearn a woman's voice that he knowed, and then he would let loose on her fambly, going backwards to her grandfathers and downwards to her children's children. If her father had once stolen a hog, or her husband done any disgrace that got found out on him, Hank would put it all into his gineral remarks with trimmings onto it.[1]

Anyone who has read *Huck Finn* will be immediately reminded of the scene in which Pap Finn launches into a tirade against the government for allowing a Negro to vote, then barks both shins on a tub of salt pork; and ends by outcussing Old Sowberry Hagan in his best days.

The use of an unsophisticated narrator is only one of several similarities between the two novels. Doc Kirby is a mild version of the

Duke and Dauphin. He is a con man who will do almost anything to "make a buck." Interestingly, after his early enthusiasm for the scheme, Marquis has him reject selling a magic elixir which is guaranteed to turn blacks white. The Duke and Dauphin have no scruples about selling Jim or cheating the Wilkes girls. Yet, since Doc Kirby is Danny's father, he must be treated somewhat sentimentally. Thus, after Danny falls in love with Martha, Doc, who is drunk, delivers a highly rhetorical bit of advice: "If she's fool enough to love you, treat her well—treat her well. For if you don't, you can never run away from the hell you'll carry in your own heart."[2] Whenever the Duke and Dauphin use language like this, there is certain to be a masterful swindle in the making.

Insofar as *Danny's Own Story* presents a view of American society, it is fairly negative. Marquis treats small towns and their citizens with much of Twain's sarcasm. Again, however, the cruelty is not so pronounced as in *Huck Finn*. Like Twain, Marquis sees the hypocrisy of a Southern gentility who could criticize the Night-Riders in Tennessee in the early twentieth century for acts of violence and, at the same time, defend the Ku Klux Klan's violence as being necessary for keeping the blacks in their place. In a touch reminiscent of Twain's handling of the Grangerford-Shepherdson feud, the old gentleman who defends the Klan is described as being " . . . very quiet and peaceful . . . " but " . . . so dern foolish about law and order he had to up and shoot a man, about fifteen years ago, who hearn him talking that-a-way and said he reminded him of a Boston school teacher."[3]

Later in the novel, Danny and Doc Kirby are taken captive in rural Georgia by a group of men who intend to execute them for inciting the local black population. This incident culminates in a trial. Marquis describes the members of the court very sarcastically. They invoke their rights as Anglo-Saxons to put down any threat to white supremacy by whatever means are necessary, insisting that they represent "communal sense."[4] Doc Kirby insists that it is murder, even offering to be killed if Danny can go free. At this point, Colonel Tom Buckner, who is the brother of Danny's real mother and, of course, Kirby's brother-in-law, arrives to stand up to the mob. He rejects the idea of a higher law, insisting that if lynching doesn't stop, more and more innocent people will be involved. Finally, he declares that the group will have to kill him to get Doc Kirby and Danny. The group breaks up; Doc tells Danny that Colonel Tom is real "quality."[5] Again, this scene lacks the power of Colonel Sherburne holding off and deriding the lynch mob in *Huck Finn*. The mob isn't as large; the feeling of violence isn't so pronounced and Colonel Tom's speech is pallid compared to Colonel Sherburne's fiery denunciation.

The conclusions of the two novels are strikingly different. Huck announces his decision to run from civilization, leaving unresolved tensions for the reader, whereas the last lines of *Danny's Own Story*, spoken by Danny to his real mother, are, " ... I can understand why I have been feeling drawed to you for quite a spell. I'm him."[6] After revealing his identity, Danny has no fear of the future or of civilization.

On the whole, Christopher Morley's evaluation of *Danny's Own Story* is accurate: " ... *Danny's Own Story* is much too obviously Mark Twain material. It is written with savor and charm, but the memory of Huck Finn and Tom Sawyer keeps blurring the reader's focus."[7] The novel is still enjoyable as light reading, but it gives little indication of Marquis's real ability as a writer, comic or otherwise.

II The Cruise of the Jasper B.

Marquis's second novel, *The Cruise of the Jasper B.*, was published in 1916, the same year as *Hermione and Her Little Group of Serious Thinkers*. As a novel, it is hardly distinguished. However, as a burlesque of the swashbuckling romances of Dumas and such popular American writers as Richard Harding Davis and George Barr McCutcheon, it is successful. It also owes something to *Don Quixote* and Robinson's "Miniver Cheevy" because the main character in the novel, Clement Cleggett, is totally out of step with the twentieth century.

Since the humorous effectiveness of the novel depends largely on the use of a hopelessly involved plot, it is necessary to summarize what actually happens. Clement J. Cleggett, a copy reader on a New York newspaper,[8] is a devotee of the swashbuckling romances written by Dumas and others. After inheriting $500,000 from an uncle, he quits his job, at the same time challenging his managing editor to a duel. It should be added that the managing editor is later demoted to being an assistant janitor at a school of journalism. Clegett then decides to buy a ship and sail to China where he will undoubtedly have adventures. He also burns the manuscript of a romantic novel he has been writing: "Why should anyone write anything who is free to live?"[9] Cleggett next discovers the hull of the *Jasper B.* in a canal near Freeport, Long Island. He buys the ship from a Captain Abernathy. At this point, Cleggett becomes involved with a very sinister man named Logan Black who, along with his gang, tries to come aboard the *Jasper B.* The treatment of Logan Black, who wears a scarf pin in the likeness of a skull, is typical of the mock-romantic tone of the novel.

Logan retires to Morris's Road House, located very near the *Jasper B.*, although it is quite clear he will be back. Shortly thereafter, a beautiful young woman arrives at the *Jasper B.* accompanied by a Pomeranian dog, a man named Elmer, and a long box for which, she insists, she must have ice. When the ice is supplied, Lady Agatha, the young woman's real name, relates her melodramatic story. She is the widow of Sir Archibald Fairhaven, who was one of the most conservative men in England. Since Lady Agatha is a militant suffragette, she did not fit very well into her late husband's family. After his death, she was persecuted by Reginald Maltravers, the illegitimate son of her late husband's brother. When Maltravers follows her to America, she hires Elmer, a reformed convict, as a bodyguard. Elmer sends two friends to "discourage" Maltravers. They bring a long box to Lady Agatha who assumes it contains Maltravers's body. Lady Agatha has been carrying the box around New York, uncertain about her future course. The ice is, of course, being used to preserve Maltravers.

By this time, Cleggett and Lady Agatha are in love. He vows to protect her and the box at all costs. The remainder of the novel becomes more and more complex as Cleggett and the men he has hired to man the *Jasper B.* on its voyage to the Orient are drawn into several pitched battles involving cutlasses and other weapons with Logan Black and his gang. Cleggett is aided by Wilton Barnstable, a master detective, who is treated very sarcastically by Marquis. Logan Black, who has hidden counterfeiting equipment in the box that supposedly contains Maltravers, is finally defeated. As a man of honor, Cleggett offers to fight a duel with Black. Of course, Cleggett is a master swordsman. To avoid being killed, Black escapes through a secret passage between the *Jasper B.* and Morris's Road House. Cleggett pursues him and finds the master criminal has bled to death.

As one would expect, the novel is resolved romantically. Cleggett and Lady Agatha are married. They have four sons, named D'Artagnan, Athos, Porthos, and Aramis. Cleggett becomes even wealthier by taking a tip on the stock market from his barber. The final chapter finds Cleggett and his family living on the Claiborne estates in England. The King wants him to take the title of Earl of Claiborne; however, Cleggett refuses since the honor of being an American citizen is higher than what the King offers. At the end of the novel, Cleggett offers to let the King make Athos the Earl of Claiborne.

The complicated plot, really a series of connected episodes designed to show the hero and heroine in the best possible light, certainly resembles Dumas, Davis, and McCutcheon. Undoubtedly, Marquis was familiar with the popular romantic novels and stories of Richard Harding Davis which featured American men triumphing over all odds in all parts of the world. It is also interesting to note that, about the time Marquis published this novel, Douglas Fairbanks was starring in a series of films in which he portrayed the self-reliant, very vital American male who could resolve any and all problems.

As if the plot is not ridiculous enough, Marquis emphasizes his burlesque by the use of chapter titles: "A Bright Blade Leaps from a Rusty Scabbard," "A Schooner, a Skipper, and a Skull," "Beauty in Distress," "First Blood for Cleggett," "A Flame Leaps Out of the Dark," "Romance Regnant," a chapter which, in its entirety, reads, "Cleggett kissed her. . . ."[10]

Throughout the novel, Marquis also uses overblown, melodramatic language; for instance, when Lady Agatha tries to stop Cleggett from fighting the duel with Logan Black, Cleggett replies that he must defend his honor:

"I have never truly lived in this age. I have lived in the past; I have held to the dream; I have believed in the bright adventure; . . . I would rather be mad with a Don Quixote than sane with Andrew Carnegie and pile up platitudes and dollars. . . ."

She had listened, mute and immobile, and as he spoke the red sun made a sudden glory of her hair. . . .

"If you are killed," she said, "it will have been more than most women ever get, to have known and loved you for two days."

"Two days?" he said. "Forever!"

"Forever!" she said.[12]

Many readers would sympathize with Cleggett's choice of Cervantes over Carnegie. Yet, to take this passage or any other passage in the novel seriously would be to destroy the broad humor—the one saving grace in this novel.

Marquis also uses minor characters for humorous effect: Guiseppe

Jones, an anarchist free-verse poet; Wilton Barnstable, a master detective who is more concerned with good newspaper coverage than anything else (he is strikingly similar to the chief detective in Twain's "The Stolen White Elephant"); and Miss Genevive Pringle, a spinster from New Jersey who is trying to recover a box of plum preserves made from a plum tree under which she once received a proposal of marriage.

Although *The Cruise of the Jasper B.* is not a success as a novel, it is entertaining to read, especially if one is familiar with the type of novel Marquis is burlesquing. Marquis continued to use the burlesque novel in his newspaper columns; however, his next novel, published in 1930, was not at all similar to his past novels.

III Off the Arm

By the time *Off the Arm* was published in 1930, Marquis was supporting himself as a free-lance writer. This may partially explain why he had not published a novel since 1916. *Off the Arm* grew out of his experiences in Hollywood. Marquis was never as fully involved with the movie business as Nathanael West and F. Scott Fitzgerald and his novel is vastly inferior to either *The Day of the Locust* or *The Last Tycoon,* mainly because it does not attempt to get beneath the surface of Hollywood.

The novel has three main characters: Gerald Wadleigh, a popular novelist; Hugh Cass, a writer who believes he is a genius; and Sally Cass, who is married to Hugh for part of the novel. *Off the Arm* begins in Paris, during the 1920s, when Wadleigh is taken home by Hugh Cass to meet Sally, a very youthful, frank, and appealing young woman who puts up with her husband's pretensions because she loves him. Cass is the leader of a group of "serious thinkers" who will praise him as long as the food and liquor hold out.[12] During the course of the evening, Hugh makes fun of Sally's paintings. She attempts suicide by jumping in the Seine, but is stopped by Wadleigh who has followed her. They return to Cass's apartment to find Hugh writing a free-verse poem, unaware that his wife has been absent.

Two years later, Cass has written a popular autobiographical novel. Wadleigh meets him, learns he and Sally have been divorced and finds Sally working in a Greenwich Village café run by an immense black woman named Aunt Caroline. Wadleigh declares his love for Sally, but it is quite clear that she still loves Hugh Cass.

Wadleigh then gets a job in Hollywood where Cass has already gone to supervise the filming of his novel. Unfortunately, by the time Wadleigh gets to Hollywood, Cass has succeeded in antagonizing the film industry. He is broke, living in a deserted garage. Wadleigh agrees to support Cass while he finishes his new novel, which Wadleigh believes is a work of genius.

Shortly after this, Wadleigh discovers that Sally has become a movie star. He visits her, finds that she still loves Cass, but is going to marry her director, mainly because of her career. On the wedding day, Cass, who has completed his novel, appears, has a tremendous fight with the director, defeats him, and is reunited with Sally. In the last chapter, Sally is in control; she will make a few more movies, save her money, go back to New York and open a tea room. If Hugh succeeds as a highbrow writer, fine. If not, he will be the headwaiter at the new tea room. Sally has been a waitress herself and is sure she can make the tea room succeed. (The title of the novel comes from her description of her work as a waitress.) Wadleigh's last thoughts are not optimistic:

I looked at the unconscious Cass with a certain amount of sympathy. His only hope is another successful novel—and his ideas are getting more highbrow, more remote from popular acceptance, every month.[13]

Marquis surrounds this rather thin, undemanding plot with some satirical jabs at favorite targets, particularly fake highbrows. As the last lines of the novel suggest, Marquis's sympathies are with the writer who appeals to a popular, mass audience. The little group of serious thinkers surrounding Cass at the beginning of the novel are as phony as Hermione and her group. They dote over a Russian who really wants to be a bond salesman in New York. They spend their time talking about art, instead of creating it. Cass does have talent, but is also very vain, taking himself much too seriously. In Hollywood, Wadleigh admires those who actually work at making movies, who know something about them, whether they are writers, cameramen, directors, or stunt men.

Sally is the most genuine character in the novel; she uses whatever talent she has fully, but doesn't try to put on a false front—at least not with her friends. Yet, when she becomes a star, she is called Iñes Del Arroyo. To make her glamorous, the studio creates an old California Spanish family for her, complete with a mother who says virtually nothing and spends most of her time asleep.

One other point of interest in *Off the Arm* is Marquis's use of real people. When Wadleigh arrives in Hollywood, he is taken, by a friend, to Douglas Fairbanks's dressing room. In this rather lavish setting, he also meets Charlie Chaplin, who is swimming in Fairbanks's pool. When Wadleigh asks Charlie what he thinks of talking pictures, Chaplin replies by pretending to drown himself.

By any standard, *Off the Arm* is an inferior work, but it does give Marquis a chance to hit some familiar targets and to caricature some of his friends and himself, for Wadleigh is undoubtedly supposed to represent Marquis as an overweight, middle-aged, popular writer. One wishes Marquis would have been able to write a more complex, more humorous novel about Hollywood, but by the early 1930s he was battling bad health and an increasingly difficult financial situation that necessitated, far too often, quantity instead of quality.

IV   Sons of the Puritans

While Marquis did not live to see his last novel, *Sons of the Puritans*, published, or even completed, there is no doubt that he worked on it for years. In fact, he published parts of the novel as short stories over the last decade of his life. There is also no doubt that he considered *Sons of the Puritans* his masterpiece, the big book he believed would secure his reputation with the critics. When it became apparent that Marquis would not be able to finish the novel even though he desperately needed the income it would provide, there were attempts to have one of his friends, either Elmer Davis or Homer Croy, finish it for him. Although Marquis evidently agreed with the idea, Davis and Croy felt it would be inappropriate. The novel was unfinished at the time of his death and was finally published in 1939 with a preface by Christopher Morley and Marquis's notes for how the novel should be completed.

Without a doubt, *Sons of the Puritans* is Marquis's best novel, even though incomplete. It has a depth missing in his other novels, although, by 1939, the subject matter would have been quite familiar. The use of a small Midwestern town, Hazelton, Illinois, " . . . constitutes a late but memorable chapter in the revolt from the village."[14] The reviews at the time of publication were generally favorable; Henry S. Canby thought the completed novel would have been an American classic.[15] The *New York Times* reviewer was upset because more of Marquis's notes about the novel weren't included, but thought the novel reconciled the gaiety of Archy and the tragic poetry of his play *The Dark Hours*.[16] One of the more interesting reviews took a rather sentimental view of the novel, finding it ". . . as fascinating as an old-fashioned scrap bag . . . it affords the interest of a treasure hunt and the nostalgic charm of a letter from home."[17]

Hazelton is obviously Walnut, Illinois, just as St. Petersburg is obviously Hannibal, Missouri. The novel takes place approximately forty years earlier, allowing Marquis to recreate Walnut as he remembered it when he had last lived there. Generally, Hazelton is similar to Gopher Prairie, Spoon River, and Winesburg. It is dominated by religion and an oppressive provincialism.

The central character is Jack Stevens, an orphan whose father was the Reverend John Knox Stevens, a famous fire and brimstone preacher. Jack is being raised by his aunt, Matilda Stevens, a spinster, who bears considerable resemblance to Tom Sawyer's Aunt Polly. Raising Jack largely by "hand," she infuses him with the highly puritanical religion common to both Hazelton churches, the Hill Church and the White Church. Because Aunt Matilda is a staunch member of the White Church, Jack grows up with strong religious convictions, which are tested by his encounters with Mister Splain, a tinker, who rooms at Aunt Matilda's. Mr. Splain drinks heavily and takes a generally hedonistic view of life. When drunk, he sings a monotonous ballad about how he rode with Jesse James.

A much stronger influence on Jack is Dr. Stuart, a neighbor of the Stevens whose characterization is very probably based on Marquis's father. He is a free thinker who encourages Jack along similar lines. He also encourages Jack to use his rather extensive library. Dr. Stuart's daughter, Barbara, dislikes the town, although she and Jack are drawn toward one another. Evidently, based on his notes, Marquis planned to have Barbara and Jack meet in New York, fall in love, and marry. Dr. Stuart becomes a morphine addict, allows himself to be baptized into membership in the Hill Church, then, as his dying act, turns on the church members and orders them from his house.

When Jack finishes high school, he decides to attend Calvin College (obviously modeled after Knox College) to become a minister. Jack attends Calvin College, an intensely moralistic and religious school, for two years. Although Marquis handles the college setting with a good deal of conventional humor, including the use of the college widow, the major point of this portion of the novel is Jack's rebellion against the repressive atmosphere he finds at Calvin The only teacher Jack cares for is Dr. Carrington Dalrymple, D. D., a young rather liberal University of Chicago graduate who teaches English. After his second year at Calvin, Jack returns to Hazelton for the summer, rather uncertain about what he wants to do with his life. He is no longer interested in becoming a minister.

At this point, Marquis was faced with the problem of getting Jack and Barbara Stuart from Hazelton to New York. Barbara is completely alienated from the town because of its treatment of her father. Jack becomes enraged at the funeral of Cherry Salters, the town prostitute, who has been killed in a fight between her father, Clem, a ne'er-do-well who lives on the edge of the swamp, and a group of men who want to run Clem and Cherry out of town. At Cherry's funeral, when the minister tries to make Cherry into a symbol of the wages of sin, Jack interrupts the service to lash out at the minister and the congregation.

Based on his rather detailed notes, included at the end of the novel, Marquis intended to have Jack and Barbara both get to New York and become involved with the literary and artistic movements in Greenwich Village in the pre-World War I period. By the time the United States entered the war in 1917, Jack would be disgusted with radicals and would enlist. Barbara and Jack were to meet in New York, fall in love, get married shortly before he goes overseas. Marquis appears to have decided that Jack would be killed in combat with his dying words being "God was bald-headed," which would connect the opening chapter of the novel where young Jack questions Aunt Matilda about why there can't be a God who isn't bald-headed. However, Marquis did leave one other possible ending in which Jack lives, Barbara decides that she needs a God, Jack declares he can get along without God or religion, and both are very happy.

As with Marquis's other novels, *Sons of the Puritans* is not memorable for its plot. It is episodic, really a series of incidents showing Jack's gradual movement away from Hazelton. Even if Marquis had completed the novel, it is doubtful if the form would have changed much. It is the depiction of Hazelton and Jack's childhood environment that gives *Sons of the Puritans* its quality.

Generally, Marquis's treatment of Hazelton is negative. Intellectually and culturally, it is very shallow. There is no need to struggle, to have ideas. Although there is really little doctrinal difference between the two Hazelton churches, this does not lessen the importance of being a staunch member of one:

> The very fact that there was no sharp divergences of belief gave the little struggles between the two churches an aspect something less than dignified. If the Hill Church gave an ice-cream social or a chicken dinner, the White Church, within a fortnight, endeavored to outdo it. If the White Church imported a traveling evangelist and started in to save the community from perdition, the Hill Church also began a series of revival meetings. . . . [18]

Marquis's portrayal of Hazelton as provincial, narrow-minded, and prejudiced, especially toward Catholics, would hardly have been shocking by the late 1930s. Most of the characters in the novel are quite conventional, but handled well; the free-thinking doctor; the spinster teacher who writes poems about the recently deceased for the local paper and who is treated like Emmeline Grangerford, even to the extent of having the same first name; the minister's daughter who wants desperately to rebel against her father's way of life. In his preface to the novel, Christopher Morley compares Marquis to Twain, and suggests what Marquis actually accomplished in the novel:

> I have written elsewhere of the strong temperamental affinity between Don Marquis and Mark Twain. It is impossible to consider the novel with the respect it deserves without seeing that it follows a kind of Mark Twain pattern; even in its crisp and lucid, persuasive style. . . . It must be remembered that the two men, at forty years apart, were raised in somewhat similar scenes and used kindred material.
>
> Marquis's greatest achievement here is of course 'Hazelton' itself, . . . His boyhood observations, and his acutely conceived microcosm of human types, had not been deformed or sophisticated by any later scrutiny. . . . The hypocrisies of Hazelton are lovingly enjoyed because they are the hypocrisies of all the world. [19]

Whether or not greater sophistication would have been a hindrance to the novel is certainly debatable. Yet, Morley's insistence on the universality of Hazelton is supported by a reading of the novel. *Sons of the Puritans* lacks the poetic intensity of *Winesburg, Ohio*, or the satiric details of *Main Street*. Yet, it should be considered a successful, if late, addition to the revolt against the village. If Marquis had lived to complete it, it would have been a revolt against hypocrisy and pretension everywhere.

After reading Marquis's four novels, a careful reader must conclude that he was not an important force in the development of the American novel. About the most that can be said is that all of his novels, with the exception of *Off the Arm*, are still entertaining to read. To someone familiar with Marquis's other works, the style and themes he uses are quite familiar.

In *Danny's Own Story*, Marquis is not attempting to write a serious novel. He clearly wants to pay homage to Twain, and in doing so he reveals his skill at using the vernacular and his skill at handling the picaresque form. *The Cruise of the Jasper B.* is even lighter weight than *Danny's Own Story*. Marquis intends nothing more than a lighthearted spoof of the swashbuckling romances so popular in the early twentieth century. The novel does show Marquis's skill at parody, but offers little evidence of his skill as a novelist. It is difficult to point to any clearly defined intentions behind *Off the Arm*. Marquis is obviously disenchanted with pseudoartists who spend more time talking than creating, but the novel demonstrates no novelistic ability and very little evidence of Marquis's skill as a humorist. Only *Sons of the Puritans* is clearly intended to be a serious novel. Marquis obviously wanted it to be his magnum opus. Certainly it is the only one of his novels that can be taken seriously as a novel. If he had lived to complete it, he might well be remembered as an American novelist.

CHAPTER 7

Marquis as Storyteller

B ESIDES publishing parts of his novels as short stories, Marquis also published six collections of short stories during his lifetime: *Carter and Other People* (1921); *The Revolt of the Oyster* (1922); *When the Turtles Sing and Other Unusual Tales* (1928); *A Variety of People* (1929); *Chapters for the Orthodox* (made up largely of short stories) (1934); and *Sun Dial Time* (1936). With one exception, "Country Doctor," I will say nothing in this chapter of Marquis's many uncollected stories from various periodicals. After having read them all, I believe only "Country Doctor" is equal to the stories considered in this chapter. A few are as good as some of the inferior collected stories, but degrees of inferiority are hardly worth consideration.

I   The Humorous Stories

While many of Marquis's short stories suffer from a rather heavy dose of O. Henry, at his best, Marquis wrote a number of stories that have been unjustly neglected by both the critics and the reading public. As with his poetry, most of his successful stories are humorous. Although Marquis does not limit himself to one time period or setting, he does use some characters and settings in a number of stories. Among his most successful humorous stories are those narrated by Tim O'Meara, a Brooklyn Irishman, who is determined that his sons will fully appreciate their ancestors' greatness. At the beginning of each story, Tim's two sons goad him into telling a story about how an O'Meara was at the center of some famous past historical event. For instance, Homer was really an O'Meara whose name was changed in translation. He led a group of Irish soldiers to Troy, where, in order to become involved in the war, they pretended to be gods from Mt. Olympus. O'Meara falls in love with Helen of Troy and defeats both Greeks and Trojans to save her. Later, when an Irishman named O'Day shows up at O'Meara's palace in Ireland, needing a story to explain to his wife why he's been gone for so long, O'Meara writes *The Odyssey* for him. In another story, an O'Meara helps Napoleon and in still another story, an O'Meara uses the fact that Mary Queen of Scots and Queen Elizabeth both love him to help the Irish. Another O'Meara even enlists the aid of a whale to help the *Mayflower* reach the new world. In all the O'Meara stories, Marquis uses exaggeration effectively, is able to mildly ridicule famous figures of the past, and manages to use ethnic stereotypes in generally good taste.

In the O'Meara stories and elsewhere, Marquis was quite fond of using the frame for telling a comic story.[1] As with Twain, it allows the author to establish a comic narrator as well as tell a humorous story. How the story is told becomes more important than what the story is actually about. Thus, Marquis does not have to rely too heavily on plotting; when he does, the result is, very often, an inferior story.

For instance, in "Rooney's Touchdown," Marquis barely uses a frame, but it is enough for the desired effect. The story is told by Joe, a friendly waiter in a restaurant, who begins by complaining about how soft modern football has become: "When I played the game it was some different from wood-tag and pump-pump-pull-away. It's went to the dogs."[2] He then admits to Marquis that he once played football for the Kingstown, Illinois, Athletic Association in the late 1890s, having joined the team instead of serving time for vagrancy. (Here, Marquis was probably drawing on his recollections of the brief time he spent trying to play football for Knox College in the late 1890s.) The Kingstown team is a mixture of ex-college players and recruits from various walks of life.

The story centers around the big Thanksgiving Day game with Lincoln College. Shortly before the game, Jerry Coakley, Kingstown's best player, disappears; the Kingstown coach comes up with two new players, a "Austro-Hungarian Dutchman" and a Mr. Rooney who is never fully introduced to the team, but Joe, who believes Rooney is Irish because of the name and his red whiskers, says " . . . he must have learned to play football by carrying the hod."[3] On the day of the game, Jerry Coakley appears with the Lincoln team; the game soon becomes a free-for-all with no officials or rules.

Rooney plays very well, blocking and tackling ferociously, even stopping Jerry Coakley cold. In the second half, there is a wild free-for-all; from it, Rooney emerges with the football and "ambles" down the field instead of running. The whole Lincoln team tries to tackle him but fails. It appears Kingstown has won the game; however, Joe hesitates in revealing the outcome since he is uncertain his audience will believe it. Mr. Rooney climbs the goalposts and tries to crack the ball open on the crossbars, thinking it is a cocoanut. "He was a regular ape; he was one of these here Orang-Outang baboons! Yes sir, a regular gosh-darned Darwinian gorilla!"[4] The story closes, not with Joe insisting on the reader believing his story as much as with Joe meditating on what has happened to the game:

"I notice," he said, sarcastically, "Princeton had a couple of men hurt yesterday in the Yale game. Well, accidents is bound to happen even in ring-around-the-rosy or prisoner's base. . . ."[5]

This final comment turns the reader back to Joe's real purpose in telling the story—a demonstration of how football has become dandified. Actually, the Kingstown-Lincoln game is not far removed from the violence of Sut Lovingood and other frontier humor. However, unlike Sut, the violence is cloaked in nostalgia as Joe is obviously looking back on what he believes were the good old days.

There are many other stories by Marquis that use the frame with varied degrees of success. The stories narrated by Clem Hawley, which were discussed earlier, use the frame with considerable skill. Yet, of all Marquis's stories, none uses the devices of traditional American humor more successfully than "The Saddest Man." Here, he begins with three men sitting in front of a general store in Hazelton, Illinois, chewing tobacco and trying to outdo one another in telling stories. Hennery McNabb, the owner of the store and the village atheist (his character is borrowed from *The Old Soak*), and Ben Grevis, the village grave digger, find the third man, a stranger, very sad-looking. However, Hennery insists that he once knew a sadder man.

The next part of the story is Hennery's tale of Bud Peevy. Peevy claims to have won the 1896 presidential election for McKinley by casting the deciding vote in a district of Kentucky. In order to get to the polls, he negotiates a twelve mile trip over the hills on foot with only three pints of "corn likker" for stimulus. Bud's trip uses many of the devices of Southwest humor. For example, all the rivers are flooding because of heavy rains:

But Bud, he allows he is the best swimmer in Kentucky, and when he comes to a stream he takes a swig of corn likker and jumps in and swims acrost, boots and all—for he was runnin' in his big cowhides, strikin' sparks of fire from the mountains with every leap he made.[6]

Besides high water, Bud is harassed by Democrats who shoot at him continually. He defeats two men in a knife fight, fights a "whole pas-sell" of rattlesnakes, and faces two hurricane-maddened bears. After killing one bear, Bud rides the other to the polling place, arriving with ten seconds to spare. His one vote carries the electoral district for McKinley, which, in turn, carries the state of Kentucky for McKinley. According to Bud, this encouraged two or three other states, who kept their polls open, to go for McKinley, assuring his election.

Because he won for McKinley, Bud becomes very self-important until he fights Zeke Humphries whose farm has just been declared the geographical center of the United States. Bud makes a great deal of noise, in frontier-boasting fashion, but Zeke defeats him easily; Bud is humiliated, becomes a laughing stock and is totally crushed when his only daughter marries Zeke Humphries.

Ben Grevis and the stranger admit that Bud is sad, but insist that real sadness can only come when a woman is involved. Ben Grevis declares that something much sadder than what happened to Bud Peevy is happening near Hazelton. He describes the Widder Watson, who lives in the woods, has buried four or five husbands, and is sad because her greatest wish can't come true. She has given her eighteen or twenty children names taken from the many almanacs she gets at drug stores; the oldest daughter is named Zodiac; there are also Peruna, Tonsillitis, Whitsuntide, and many more. Now, she has the perfect name for a new child and no husband. Ben believes if she made herself a little more attractive she might get a husband but, at present, he considers her the saddest sight in Illinois.

Finally, the stranger, who has become sadder and sadder, admits that both previous stories have been sad, but he is sadder than either Bud Peevy or the Widder Watson. Earlier in life, he was a sideshow freak; he could be the India Rubber Man because of his unusual skin, the Living Skeleton, because he is so tall and thin or a glass eater. He preferred being the India Rubber Man because it required the greatest genius and the most practice. While with a circus, he fell in love with Siamese twins named Hetty and Netty Jones. He wanted to marry both of them, but they considered this immoral, insisting that he must choose between them. Finally, in order to solve the problem, an oper-ation was performed to separate Hetty and Netty. Unfortunately, after separation neither loves the India Rubber Man—both marry someone else. For years, he has lived with melancholy sorrow. Then, as he admits, five days ago, he changed melancholy sorrow to bitter sorrow by marrying. Ben Grevis doesn't believe that the stranger, although sad, is any sadder than the Widder Watson:

> The stranger spat colourfully into the road, and again the faint semblance of a smile, a bitter smile, wreathed itself about his mouth.
> "Yes, I be!" he said, "I be a sadder person than the Widder Watson. It was her I married!"[7]

The conclusion is a little forced, showing Marquis's fondness for O. Henry endings. Yet, the story does certainly show his skill as a humorous storyteller. The plot is insignificant; actually, it is three stories tied around a common theme. It could easily have been told by Twain or some earlier humorist. Bud Peevy's epic race to vote is right out of Davy Crockett and other frontier humor. I find Marquis at his best in stories such as "The Saddest Man" where he uses familiar techniques with great skill.

Another later story, published in 1929, "The Ancient Mariner," uses the frame to deflate Hollywood, a subject Marquis did not often deal with in his fiction. The Ancient Mariner is Captain Samuel Billings, a retired sea captain who possesses a very distinguished white beard. Becoming interested in Captain Billings, Marquis follows him into Gorman's Babylonian Theater. In connection with the current feature, a biblical epic called *The Patriarch*, the theater is presenting a pageant featuring real camels, elephants, and zebras with Captain Billings and two other old men with white beards, riding the camels, portraying patriarchs. Marquis introduces himself to Captain Billings who is bitter because the scenario he has written about his life has been rejected by the major studios. After their friendship develops, Captain Billings gives Marquis the scenario to read.

Billings' scenario itself satirizes the movies. Marquis apparently never felt he was allowed to use his talents correctly by whatever studio had him under contract. Captain Billings's scenario may well be his revenge for the frustration he had found in Hollywood.

The main story line of the scenario deals with Captain Billings's love for Miss Nancy Lane. Captain Billings is about to depart on another trip to the South Seas and agrees to find Nancy's long-lost father who vanished in the South Seas more than twenty years ago. Nancy agrees to marry him if he brings back her father. After fights with pirates and cannibals and proposals of marriage from native queens when his ship is wrecked, Captain Billings is cast ashore on a desert island with no

food of any sort available. In the same storm, another ship is wrecked
and its captain, Bully Jackson, takes refuge on the same island. Jackson
is a bad man; he has been a " . . . pirate, smuggler, kidnapper, murderer, gambler, black mailer, bigamist, robber and so forth. . . ."[8]
Faced with starvation, Jackson suggests that they follow the old rule of
the sea that castaways always eat the fattest of the group. Unable to
agree who is the fattest, the two play poker; although Bully Jackson is
a card-sharp, Billings wins. Captain Billings doesn't believe it would be
a good idea to show him eating Bully Jackson, although he does. So,
the scene shifts to his being rescued by a British gunboat. The British
captain tells Billings he has acted correctly by eating Jackson. When
the name is revealed, he also tells Billings that there is almost a half-
million dollars in rewards being offered for Jackson. Unfortunately,
Captain Billings has no proof that he ate Jackson, so he is unable to
collect the reward.

Finally, he arrives to claim Nancy. However, when Nancy's mother
hears a description of Bully Jackson's tattoos, she states that Jackson
was her long-lost husband. Although her mother defends Billings,
Nancy refuses to marry him; instead, she marries Billings's arch rival,
sending a broken Captain Billings into the world.

After reading the scenario, Marquis tells the Captain that it is too
sad, too tragic. Billings then produces a happy ending he has written
in which Nancy is considerably younger; her mother is a very attractive woman of about thirty-one who marries Captain Billings. In this
version, they find enough evidence to collect the rewards for Bully
Jackson.

At this point, Marquis imposes the frame again. Captain Billings's
wife, a burly woman named Nancy, appears in a rage because he has
been missing for three months. She threatens to take him to Iowa to
plow corn. As they disappear, Marquis ends the story with a question
about Billings's beard:

Was its maritime quality solely a matter of aspiration, created by the salty
spirit of a baffled mariner, or was there some foundation of fact underlying
his lively fancy?[9]

Besides the obvious implication that Marquis has been the victim of
Billings's imagination, it is clear that whether the story is true or not
makes little difference in Hollywood where there is a thin line, if any,
between truth and fantasy, with a happy ending always available.

Throughout the scenario, Captain Billings offers suggestions to whoever will film the epic of his life:

> You got a great chance here to run in a lot of pictures of Iseland Beauties, you could show Captain Billings teaching them to wear clothes, some break down and promise to join the Church and wear clothes, some do not, if it costs too much to send to the iselands for a lot of Dusky Beauties you can find lots of extra girls around Hollywood out of work would be willing to tan their-selves up a little and would wear any quantity of clothes or not as you might dessignate, there is a chance here for some nice dances and songs. [10]

Another good touch, Billings feels, is having himself, Nancy, and other characters speak in verse during especially romantic or emotional moments.

By the end of the scenario, the reader is not convinced that any of it really happened, but is convinced that it could be filmed. In fact, taking out the cannibalism, it has been filmed many times. Again, Marquis realizes that how a story is told, not what it is about, is the key. He destroys the idea of plot importance by offering two endings and then casting doubts on both of them.

Nowhere in Marquis's humorous stories is the influence of Twain more obvious than in a series of five stories published in *The Revolt of the Oyster*. The stories all take place in Hazelton, Illinois. One of the stories, "The Kidnapping of Bill Patterson," is narrated by a boy named Freckles Watson. (At intervals Marquis had been using "The Diary of Freckles Watson" in his newspaper column.) At the beginning of the story, Freckles and other members of the Dalton Gang, as they call themselves, are meeting in Horsethieves Cave. They are upset because one of the boys' fathers has laughed at the gang's oath. In order to avenge themselves on the town, they decide to kidnap someone. After rejecting nearly everyone in Hazelton because some member of the gang is a relative, they decide on Bill Patterson, the town drunk. He is taken from the town jail, where he spends every weekend and is held in the cave. The gang's demand of $500 from the town for ransom is treated as a joke. Unfortunately, Bill Patterson enjoys being kidnapped since he is fed well, steals enough liquor to supply his needs, and sleeps as much as he wants. When the gang tells him that he is free, he refuses to go, threatening to inform on them if they don't treat him right. Bill's demands get more and more oppressive, including being fanned while he sleeps. Finally, after two days of drinking with

a tramp who has also decided to be kidnapped, Bill is so helpless that
the boys are able to get him back into jail. They put up notices around
town that it was all a joke by Bill Patterson to get even with the town
for the way they've treated him. Bill believes this story himself,
although when he sees members of the gang on the street, he is certain
he has seen them when he was travelling.

The other four Freckles Watson stories are told by Spot, a dog who,
in his view, has a boy named Freckles Watson. They all deal with Spot
and Freckles being forced to maintain their reputations against other
dogs and boys of the town. In one of the stories, Spot chases a runaway
circus lion who has broken into Freckles's father's drug store. Spot
thinks the lion is a dog, bites him, and chases him from the store. This
makes Spot and Freckles heroes although at the end of the story, when
Spot sees the lion in a cage, he isn't so sure he would have bitten him
if he had known the lion's true identity. (Interestingly, for years Marquis told a story of how he had confronted a circus lion in an Atlanta
bar although none of his friends was sure how much of the story to
believe.)

In writing these stories, Marquis was undoubtedly looking back at
his own boyhood in Walnut. The influence of Twain, especially *Tom
Sawyer,* and probably *Penrod* by Booth Tarkington, is too heavy for
the stories to be totally successful, but they do show a side of Marquis
not so apparent in his other stories.

The more of Marquis's stories one reads, the more one becomes convinced that he is at his best when he can forget about plotting and
concentrate on the effect of the story. This allows him to use popular
forms such as movie scenarios and melodramas for humorous effect. In
"The Glass Eater's Story," he falls back on one of his favorite devices—
a parody of temperance literature. The story begins with the ex-glass
eater named Eliphalet Vare coming home from working as an expert
oyster and clam opener in a restaurant to find that his ten-month-old
son is a victim of the weakness that runs in the Vare family. When his
wife discovers that her son is a glass eater she faints. Her glasses fall
into the crib, where the infant eats them.

In the rest of the story, Vare relates how he became a glass eater,
and how, after eating part of a stained-glass window in a church, he
was saved by his future wife and her father, a minister. The last part
of the story brings the reader back to Eliphalet, Jr. Vare and his wife
are facing the problem together, determined that their son will not fall
victim to the Glass Demon. The story ends with a challenge to those

who have so far avoided the Glass Demon: "Take Warning! You may think that you are strong—but beware of the First Glass!"[11]

II   *Nonhumorous Stories*

In turning to Marquis's nonhumorous stories, there is much less to say. Many of these stories are simply formula pieces written for the *Saturday Evening Post, Collier's,* and other magazines. In these stories, Marquis was much less free to use his imagination than in his humorous stories. Most of these stories are melodramatic to a degree, depending too heavily on a resolution that suggests O. Henry. However, a few of the nonhumorous stories are still interesting.

Perhaps the most appealing of these is "Country Doctor," a story which, for some reason, Marquis never included in any of the collections of stories published during his lifetime.[12] "Country Doctor" is obviously intended as a tribute to Dr. James Stewart Marquis, his father, who, Marquis believed, never thought his son would amount to anything. The story takes place in and near a small town in northern Illinois on a stormy night in late October. Dr. Stewart, now past eighty, has devoted his life to serving both the people in the town and the people living in the swamp near the town. Now Dr. Stewart realizes that he has a bad heart; he will not live much longer. Neither of the two younger doctors in the town is interested in taking care of the people in the swamp.

At this point, a swamp resident, Jason Tucker, arrives to announce that Myra, his wife, is nearly ready to give birth. Since Dr. Stewart delivered Myra and, later, rebuilt her face after she was kicked by a horse, he feels an obligation to be there when her child arrives. The major portion of the story deals with his epic journey through a pouring rain and flood conditions. He is forced to ford a raging river on foot, finally arriving, nearly dead, at the Tucker farm. When he arrives, he finds that young Dr. Hastings has made the trip on horseback with a broken foot. At this point, Dr. Stewart suffers a fatal heart attack and dies, happy with the knowledge that someone will take his place with the people of the swamp.

The very affectionate portrait of Dr. Stewart dominates the story with little plotting really necessary. His trip through the storm is properly epical, and his death is handled without too much sentimentalism. If the resolution is too obvious, it is still believable.

Many of Marquis's nonhumorous stories center around a love triangle or the destructive force of love. Again, unfortunately, he usually handles these themes quite conventionally, meeting the requirements of whatever magazine he was writing for. In "The Strong Grasses," a farmer overhears his wife and her lover, a young man working on the farm. He confronts them; when the young man fights back, the farmer kills him. His wife declares she will leave the next day.[13] Sherwood Anderson was drawn to similar situations in *Winesburg, Ohio;* however, he avoided the melodramatic confrontation scene which climaxes "The Strong Grasses."

Another love story, "The Magic Melody," takes place in ancient Greece, a setting Marquis also used in some humorous work. Creon, the hero, is a young man who is searching for a beautiful melody he has heard in a dream. Instead of becoming involved with worldly things, he wanders the countryside, playing his pipes, searching for the melody. Zoë, whom he loves, can't understand what has happened. Creon finally convinces her that there is a magic melody. When she reminds him of their passionate love in the past, he insists that this melody is even stronger than Aphrodite. Zoë gives up, deciding she has no reason to continue living. Marquis then has Creon meet the temptations of the world. First, he rejects a minstrel's offer to tour with him. Then, Creon becomes involved with a group of sailors who are the advance guard of an invasion fleet. When Creon senses the splendor of this fleet, the idea that one man can control all this force, he rejects his dream and the melody, believing it is better to play a role in the real world. He will gain power and wealth. He also decided that he loves Zoë passionately. Rushing to her home, Creon meets Zoë's father, who tells Creon that she has killed herself while calling his name. When Creon asks why her father didn't stop her, he says that it was from the gods—it could not be questioned. Since Creon had earlier expressed such a view about the magic melody to Zoë, Marquis obviously intends this to be rather ironical. The concluding paragraph has Creon finding the magic melody, but at a high price:

The grief of all women and all men pressed in on Creon's bosom then, and his heart broke. He took his way across the town, toward the chamber where the girl lay dead and as he went he lifted up his pipes and played. There were all things in that melody, and the people stood in their doors, and flocked from their houses, and followed him through the streets, for to each one of them the music was the core of his own life, and all the sorrow and hope and beauty of the world was there. But he never knew that he had played the music of his dream, for only when men are done with seeking do they find. Neither shall a player draw laughter from the pipes, nor tears, nor any utterance acceptable to the gods, until his heart is broken.[14]

Here Marquis is certainly expressing the high cost a poet or any true artist must pay for his gift, for being able to play the magic melody. Since Marquis wrote a good deal of lyric poetry and often expressed regret that he had not been more fully realized as a poet, this story might be an expression of his own dilemma. When the story was first published, in September 1929, Marquis had lost his first wife and his only son. Thus, the concluding sentence may reflect his own situation. In this story, Marquis also reiterates his belief in art, in creativity as a force that cannot be denied. As he grew older, he complained more and more to his friends about how he had misused his powers so that they had never been fully realized. "The Magic Melody" may be his own lament.

One of Marquis's best-known nonhumorous stories did come directly from events he witnessed personally. "Carter," originally published in *Harper's* under the title "The Mulatto," grew directly from his being in Atlanta during the race riot of September 22, 1906. Marquis tried several times without success to write a short story about the riots before "Carter" materialized.

"Carter" is an interesting story, although it never quite realizes its full potential. It is Marquis's fullest statement on the race problem and it is much more serious than the treatment of this problem in *Danny's Own Story.* Carter is seven-eighths Caucasian, but has enough black blood to make him a "nigger." He grows up hating this, realizing that when he gets into a new environment, he can pass for white. Carter also discovers that his father, a white man, was a member of one of the most distinguished Southern families.

Carter becomes more and more frustrated, wanting to succeed as a white man, since he is, to the vast majority of people, white. His one desire is to be white—if only for a year. When he goes to New York, gets work, and falls in love with a young white woman, it would seem that his prayers have been answered. Yet, he believes he must tell her that he is not all white. It becomes a great decision for him: " . . . he saw something spectacular, something histrionic, in his confession."[15] When he tells her, he can hardly dare to look at her, since he is certain

she will now reject him, but instead of reacting violently, she is more
interested in how they will get back to the city from Coney Island.
Carter cannot believe his blackness makes no difference to her:

" . . . You can marry me . . . in spite of what I am?"
"Gee! but ain't you the solemn one!" said the girl, . . . "whatcha s'pose I
care for a little thing like that?"[16]

Carter is offended by her attitude, since he believes she should care,
one way or the other. He views her as a southern white might view
her: "By God! . . . I can't have anything to do with a woman who'd
marry a nigger!"[17]
After being unable to be either black or white in New York, Carter
returns to Atlanta on the night of the 1906 riot. Marquis states that the
riot was caused by reports of white women being raped by black men,
with innocent blacks being killed. Since he is so nearly white, Carter
is safe. He observes the riot which is described very vividly by Marquis,
especially the use of a bloodthirsty dwarf as one of the mob leaders.
Carter sees the riot as an outgrowth of his own struggle between being
black and white. At this point, Carter recognizes a white man standing
nearby as his white half-brother, Willoughby Carter. Of course, Willoughby doesn't recognize Carter. After the two Carters help a
wounded Negro, Willoughby proposes to his half-brother that they,
". . . two white men of the better class . . ." [18] die in defense of the
blacks to stop the riot. Carter is thrilled to be taken for a white man
by Willoughby and agrees to die with him. When the mob appears,
they refuse to do anything to Willoughby, who protests that, in attack-
ing Carter, they are killing a white man. A member of the mob replies
that this is not the case:

"Who's a white man? Not Jerry Carter here! He wasn't any white man.
I've known him since he was a kid—he was just one of those yaller niggers."
And Carter heard it as he died.[19]

The ending is a little too contrived, but the story does present an
unresolvable problem without much glamour or sentiment. In a short
story, of course, Marquis cannot do what Twain did in *Pudd'nhead
Wilson*. He obviously doesn't want the reader to have much sympathy
for Carter, just as Twain wants no sympathy for the real Chambers.

Yet there is a basis for a real tragedy in "Carter." One comes away feeling that Marquis has not quite reached it.

Although Marquis wrote much of his fiction to meet deadlines, or to sell as soon as possible, this should not be used as an excuse. Many far greater writers had similar pressures. The quality of his short stories is very uneven. At best, he produced such stories as "The Saddest Man" or "The Ancient Mariner" utilizing the devices of traditional American humor superbly. If one must use the label "old-fashioned" when referring to Marquis's fiction, it should not be thought of as a condemnation. Marquis was not technically very innovative, except perhaps as a newspaper columnist; in fact, I do not think that technique meant much to him. When he can start someone telling a story and let the story continue unhampered in the narrator's own voice, without imposing too rigid a plot or too melodramatic a resolution, Marquis's skill as a humorous storyteller is undeniable.

CHAPTER 8

Marquis as Dramatist:
The Greatest Failure

I "Stage Struck"

AS Don Marquis admitted in an article in the *Saturday Evening Post*, "I was born stage-struck. . . . The stage to me is still the most glamorous thing in human life."[1] In the same article, he describes his experiences as an actor, including the moment of truth when he chose to remain a cub reporter in Washington, D.C., for eighteen dollars a week rather than join Otis Skinner's troupe as assistant property man. He chose literature over the stage, ". . . but with the mercenary choice, a kind of bloom left my youth; I've never been the same ingenuous, artistic spirit since."[2] In this article, Marquis is doing what an audience in the 1930s would expect from him—being funny. However, from the shows he saw as a child in Walnut, from the plays he attended with Grantland Rice in Atlanta and, of course, from a constant exposure to the theater in New York, Marquis was undoubtedly drawn to the theater.

With his great love of and exposure to the theater, why wasn't Marquis more successful as a playwright? He wrote six plays, four of which were produced on Broadway. Yet, only two of them, *The Old Soak* and *Everything's Jake*, had runs of any length and *The Old Soak* was his only real financial success as a dramatist; it was also his first Broadway production. In *The Old Soak*, Marquis does demonstrate a knowledge of popular stage techniques. However, this was, in many ways, an old-fashioned play, drawing a good deal of its effectiveness from nostalgia. Since I have discussed *The Old Soak* and *Everything's Jake* in a previous chapter, I will say little about them here. They were basically comedies, lacking much depth.

Marquis's four other plays were commercially unsuccessful. *The Dark Hours* ran for eight performances; *Out of the Sea* had only a few performances; *Master of the Revels* was never produced on Broadway. The failure of the first two plays has been commonly blamed on inadequate direction, while *Master of the Revels* was never brought to New York, on the advice of Brooks Atkinson. Marquis's sixth play, *The Skinners*, was a comedy satirizing " . . . a then current craze which Marquis had used as a target in his columning days; the wholesale quest for dukedoms—or what have you—by title-smitten wealthy Americans" (Anthony, 414). Unfortunately, *The Skinners* was given only one performance and never reached Broadway.

II   The Dark Hours

If Don Marquis had been asked what his greatest artistic disappointment had been, he almost certainly would have named the failure of *The Dark Hours*, his play dealing with the passion and crucifixion of Christ. When the Broadway production failed in 1932 through a combination of poor direction, an uneven cast, and, certainly, a far from perfect script, it nearly destroyed Marquis financially and, I believe, so demoralized him that he could never regain his earlier form as a writer.

Marquis had begun *The Dark Hours* with his first wife's enthusiastic support. Although published in 1924, after Reina's death, the play was dedicated to her. Reviews of the published play were good, with particular praise for Marquis's not allowing Christ to appear on stage and for his ability to make high drama from a very familiar story. *The Dark Hours* was certainly responsible, in part, for Marquis's being taken more seriously by critics who had dismissed him as a mere humorist.

When one reads *The Dark Hours*, he would be going against Marquis's own views to look for a radically revised or modernized version of these events. Marquis believed he was sharing a tradition, not attempting an original interpretation.[3] He presents five scenes, each coming directly from the biblical account. The first scene takes place in the house of Caiaphas, the High Priest, and describes the plans being made to capture and try Christ; it also describes the witnesses to be used against Christ. Scene Two is in the Garden of Gethsemane and is taken almost literally from the biblical account. Scene Three develops Christ's trial before the Sanhedrin, ending with his being taken to Pilate. Scene Four is at Pilate's palace, presenting Pilate, traditionally, as indecisive and weak. The final scene is, of course, at Golgotha; again, it stays very close to the biblical version.

Marquis felt strongly the *The Dark Hours* could succeed only if Christ spoke but did not appear on stage .At first, he felt that the taboo on Christ's appearance was purely religious. Later, he realized it also came from dramatic values realized by many people and cultures.[4] Anyone who has seen any of the Hollywood versions of the life of Christ, where Jesus is portrayed by an actor, would certainly agree with this view. Marquis did not, however, place the same restrictions on the other characters in the play. He admits to elaborating on the biblical Judas, Peter, John, Pilate, and Mary Magdalene. Finally, Marquis insists that when Christ spoke of his Father, he did not mean that God is the Father of us all in the same sense that He is the father of Jesus. Jesus meant that He had a unique and special relationship with God. Marquis finds Christ's insistence that he is the Son of God to be the key to the entire drama. It is this point that caused the Sanhedrin to condemn him to death without calling further witnesses.

Using these ideas, what does Marquis bring to one of the most famous events in human history? From the beginning of the play to the end, there is a sense of a few men playing out a predetermined drama in the midst of a mob that can be easily swayed by either side. In the first scene, while Caiaphas, the High Priest, and Annas, his father-in-law, are plotting Christ's downfall, believing he must be destroyed or he will bring about a conflict with Rome that will obliterate Jerusalem, the crowds of people in Jerusalem for the Passover pass by the house chanting hymns of praise to Jehovah while also showing great respect for Christ. Marquis uses the people like a chorus, allowing individual voices to speak out, but always giving the impression of a unified and brutal mob, a mob so brutal that at the moment when Pilate is appealing to Caiaphas to let Christ go, it murders two or three people who attempt to speak for Christ.

The character of Judas is given a partly original interpretation in the first scene. Judas is portrayed as a man who both loves and hates Christ. He has decided to betray Christ because he believes Christ has shown he already knows Judas will betray Him when He gave him a sop of bread as a sign. Judas goes so far as to claim that Christ has betrayed him!

... He betrayed me! ... These many weeks, yea, these months past, he has persecuted me and driven me! He has persecuted me with his knowledge of my dreams and speculations; he has taken from me my power to be myself. . . . [5]

Judas considers himself bewitched, with angels and demons fighting to control his spirit. As traditionally accepted, Judas also admits that he believed he was to be the chamberlain when Christ became King of the Jews. Now, he realizes this is not to be. Yet, the overwhelming reason for his betrayal is that " . . . we were born to be each one the other's bane. And we have felt that . . . from the first." [6] Whether one accepts this interpretation of Judas or not, it does work dramatically, making Judas a rather sympathetic character.

The other disciples are treated quite conventionally. In the Garden of Gethsemane, they bicker about who will be greatest when Christ is gone. As the Gospel of John states, Peter is willing to draw his sword and die fighting for Christ, but he is unwilling to accept being linked with Christ as a disciple. Similarly, the characters of Caiaphas, Annas, and the other priests are presented as one finds them in the Gospels.

Marquis uses several devices to sustain dramatic tension. One, mentioned previously, is the character of Judas. Another, also previously noted, is the use of the crowd as a chorus. They support Christ at first— then they turn on him. We even get the impression that their pressure intimidates Pilate so that he gives Christ to the mob. The trial before the Sanhedrin builds up to the climactic moment when Christ admits to being the Son of God. Marquis has citizens, servants, and some disciples form another chorus of sorts outside the courtroom. They comment on the trial and debate whether or not Christ did perform miracles.

The witnesses are dramatically effective. One testifies to Lazarus being raised from the dead while Peter and John, outside the courtroom, debate rescuing Christ; John insists that death means nothing to Christ. The most interesting witness is the Gadarean swineherd whose two thousand hogs were destroyed when Christ took devils from a possessed man and put them into the hogs. The swineherd is upset because he has lost his job and is now a beggar because of what he considers to be witchcraft. (Marquis was so fond of the swineherd that he made use of him again in *Chapters for the Orthodox.*) The general atmosphere at the trial is one of doubt and uncertainty, even among the disciples. When Christ admits to being the Son of God, Caiaphas tears his clothing, the mob becomes enraged, and Christ's doom is certain.

While Marquis does show proper respect toward the Passion story, this is not what gives the play whatever dramatic impact it has. His attempt to show how the events affected those who were present makes the play work as well as it does. Possibly this "sympathetic reverence" is why the last two scenes are weaker than the earlier part of the play. The scene with Pilate is almost totally conventional. Marquis manages to have Pilate say "What is truth?" and to have him wash his hands; to have him find Jesus innocent, but to have him give in to the mob. The only real dramatic power of this scene comes from the mob's attacks on anyone who attempts to defend Christ and its growing impatience and anger, finally unnerving Pilate to the point of giving in.

The final scene at Golgotha is, again, quite conventional, with the centurions casting lots for Christ's robe and Christ uttering the seven last words. Although the dialogue is conventional, Marquis does use lighting rather well in this scene, darkening the stage completely for the eclipse and then bringing in a very bright light at the moment of death and triumph. The play concludes with the centurion announcing, "Truly, this was the Son of God!" The mob, including Caiaphas and Annas, flees in terror.

There can be no doubt of Marquis's sincerity, his desire to present the Passion story as recorded. Unfortunately, when *The Dark Hours* was finally produced on Broadway in 1932, his most important point was ignored. His second wife, Marjorie Vonnegut, a highly respected actress, directed the play. For some reason, never clearly explained, she chose to represent Christ on stage. The only reason she ever gave for this was that she thought her husband was trying to be too subtle. She felt he might lose his audience if the play were produced without Christ being on stage. The play ran for only eight performances, one of which Marquis did attend, although he was quite ill at the time.

The most interesting, if not most favorable, review of *The Dark Hours* was by Joseph Wood Krutch, who reinforces the contrast between the text of the play and the Broadway production. Krutch believes that Marquis is too orthodox; he offers nothing new: " . . . almost the only novelty consists in bringing Lazarus to the foot of the Cross where he can proclaim 'there is no death' for the purpose, apparently, of pleasing the students of Christian Science." [7] Here Krutch is making a sarcastic reference to the fact that Marjorie Vonnegut Marquis was a Christian Scientist, and to the belief, never fully verified, that Marquis was himself converted to Christian Science. Krutch wants Marquis to elaborate on what the Bible leaves to our imagination; for instance, what did Judas say before he hanged himself? Krutch does find *The Dark Hours* better than most other stage or movie passion plays, but it is still uninteresting. The only interesting point is Judas's character development in the first scene which Marquis doesn't really develop fully. Krutch's basic points are undeniably accurate; however, Marquis simply didn't write the play Krutch wants him to have written.

III Out of the Sea

When Marquis wrote his next play, *Out of the Sea,* he turned to myth. Published and produced in 1927, the play is based on the Tristan-Isolde legend, which, basically, tells of the fated love between Tristan, nephew of King Mark of Lyonnesse, Cornwall, and Isolde, daughter of the King of Ireland. She heals Tristan's wounds. He returns to Lyonnesse where his uncle sends him back to Ireland to arrange a marriage between Isolde and King Mark. In Ireland, Tristan and Isolde drink a magic potion, causing them to fall deeply in love. When Mark discovers this, Tristan flees to Brittany where he marries the daughter of the Duke of Brittany. After being wounded with a poisoned weapon, Tristan sends for Isolde to heal him. If she is coming, the ship bearing her will hoist a white sail, if not, a black sail. Isolde does come, but, unfortunately, Tristan's jealous wife reports a black sail. Tristan dies in despair; Isolde commits suicide.[8]

Marquis seemed to have a good chance for a successful production as Walter Hampden, a distinguished American actor, agreed to direct the play because he thought it was beautiful and because he wanted to encourage Marquis to write more plays. Somewhat ironically, at least one review of the play blamed its failure on Hampden's inept direction, feeling that he wasn't imaginative enough to bring about the union of realism with supernatural overtones necessary for the play's success.

Out of the Sea is not as great as Hampden claimed. Yet, it is a better play than *The Dark Hours;* it has more imagination and more drama. Like *The Dark Hours*, this play depends a great deal on setting and lighting for dramatic effect. The play is set on the Cornwall coast, in approximately the same areas as Tristan and Isolde played out their drama. Although Lyonnesse vanished into the sea centuries ago, it still has a powerful effect on those who live where it once existed. *Out of the Sea* has four major characters: The first one, Arthur Logris, an

English country gentleman whose house is the major setting of the
play, knows the Tristan-Isolde story very well and is in love with the
second major character, Isobel, the young wife of Mark Tregesal. From
the beginning of the play, Isobel is identified with Isolde and the sea.
The third major character, Isobel's husband Mark Tregesal, is a powerful man of sixty. The fourth main character is John Harding, an
American poet, who wants to write about the sea and the legend.

In the first act, the link between the present and past is fully established. Almost at the beginning of the play, Harding makes much of
the spell of the sea and how the pervasive feeling of the ancient past
fills Logris's home. Logris mentions that over one thousand years ago,
there was a castle on the site of his home and the castle was on the road
to Lyonnesse. Logris is not startled at Harding's insistence that Lyonnesse has been speaking to him from the sea.

After establishing this link between past and present, Marquis inten-
sifies the drama when Mark Tregesal's yawl is wrecked, forcing Tregesal and Isobel to accept Logris's hospitality while Tregesal recovers
from injuries received during the wreck. While playing an aria from
Tristan und Isolde, Harding sees Isobel for the first time. They immediately fall in love. The first act ends with Harding insisting that Isobel
has come to him out of the sea. Logris warns him that Tregesal is a
dangerous man; however, Logris also admits that he has loved Isobel
since she was a child, and that she is a Celtic princess.

Act Two takes place in a cave overlooking the sea. Three weeks have
passed with Harding and Isobel growing even more deeply in love.
Isobel tells Harding that she was rescued from the sea as an infant and
raised by a local fisherman named Timbury. She has always been
drawn to the sea and acts unconventionally. Harding and Isobel are
discovered by Timbury who, after realizing that their love is genuine,
agrees to help them escape. The act ends with Tregesal appearing in
the cave after the others have left, suggesting that he knows what is
being planned.

Act Three, in Logris's house, centers around a confrontation between
Tregesal and Harding, during which Tregesal tells a local legend about
an ogre who torments his wife and her lover. Harding refuses to back
down although Tregesal implies that he is aware of the situation. Harding tells Tregesal that if Isobel wants to go away with him, he will take
her. In reply, Tregesal relates that while working as a miner in West
Virginia as a young man, he killed another man who tried to take his
"fancy woman" from him. After Tregesal leaves, Logris urges Harding

and Isobel to leave that night because Tregesal is dangerous. At the close of the act, Mrs. Hockin, the housekeeper, tells Isobel that she must go by herself, alone, back to where she came from.

Act Four takes place at the cave at the time Harding and Isobel are to leave. Tregesal appears instead of Harding and tells Isobel he is taking her home, insisting that he loves the elemental quality she possesses. He is determined to have a son by Isobel. Finally, when Isobel refuses to leave, he attempts to drag her physically from the cave. She stabs him with an ancient bronze bodkin she wears in her hair, claiming she has been urged to kill by the sea spirits, who come from Lyonnesse. Logris then appears, offering to take the blame for Tregesal's death. When Harding finally arrives, Isobel tells him that they must part because she has killed her husband. Harding is stunned, unable to comprehend Isobel's explanation for her act. When Isobel pleads for Harding's love and understanding, Harding rejects her, stating that his love is dead, that he cannot love her now. Isobel leaps into the sea. The concluding lines of the play shift the emphasis from tragedy to sarcasm:

LOGRIS [with quiet scorn]
    She was the sea. And what is a minor poet beside the sea?
HARDING
    I should follow her . . . I should follow her.
LOGRIS [in the same tone, turning from him]
    You won't though. You'll write a poem about it.[9]

The conclusion is reminiscent of "The Magic Melody," a Marquis story, where Creon decides, too late, to love instead of to escape from life. Here, Harding never makes this choice although it is not certain that Isobel could have broken with the sea and Lyonnesse even if she had not murdered Tregesal.

Out of the Sea uses the sea somewhat like O'Neill used it in his early plays. Throughout the play, Marquis has the wind playing an eerie melody through openings in the rocks of the cave. This, along with the overtones of the past, creates a powerful atmosphere. Tregesal and Isobel are strong characters; one can believe their conflict. Logris functions largely as a link between the past and Harding. The weakness in the play is Harding who is never quite powerful enough to be heroic. Yet, he must be heroic until the end of the play when his heroism collapses. Of course, this may be deliberate. The idea of a poet creating a beautiful poetic love which collapses when faced with the elemental forces of life would appeal to Marquis and is consistent, on a lesser level, with The Old Soak's preference for the ancient patriarchs and even Mehitabel's "toujours gai!" *Out of the Sea*, I believe, is Marquis's best written play, but not one that would appeal to a contemporary audience.

<h3 style="text-align:center">IV   Master of the Revels</h3>

In his last play, *Master of the Revels*, which mixes comedy and tragedy, Marquis again turned to the past. Published in 1934 and never produced on Broadway, the play takes place at the court of Henry VIII. In a lengthy "Dedicatory Letter" to Charles J. Bayne, a Georgia newspaperman and poet who was an old friend of Marquis's, Marquis states that he first thought of writing a play about Henry VIII twenty-five or thirty years before. His interest in writing the play was renewed by Cornelia Otis Skinner's one-woman show in which she portrayed all six wives of Henry VIII, and by Francis Hackett's biography of Henry VIII. The play was written in about three weeks, after a good deal of research, with the idea of a fall 1934 Broadway production. Marquis then states that when *The Private Life of Henry VIII*, the very popular Charles Laughton movie, appeared, plans for producing the play were dropped. Instead, Marquis published the play, believing it would be worth reading, even if it was never produced.[10]

The play was produced in an outdoor setting at Schenectady, New York, in the summer of 1935. Charles Coburn played Henry VIII and was to direct and star in the play that fall on Broadway. Brooks Atkinson's review of the outdoor production doesn't find *Master of the Revels* a great drama, but highly entertaining. In response to a letter asking whether *Master of the Revels* was good enough to be produced on Broadway, Atkinson replied in the negative.

The lack of originality in the play and the competition from the Laughton movie would have made its future on Broadway dubious. However, the reviews of the published version of the play were good; unlike Atkinson's review, they suggested that the play should reach Broadway. The reviewers did criticize the lack of movement in the play and the difficulty of portraying the characters as Marquis had written them. But the consensus was that Marquis had written a successful drama.[11]

The play develops Marquis's view of Henry VIII although he does not attempt to develop the King's character in great depth, seeing him as both an ogre and Old King Cole.[12] Actually, I believe the effectiveness of Marquis's portrayal of Henry VIII comes from his fondness for the ancient patriarchs such as Abraham, men who lived life fully, without planning too far ahead, who were both good and bad, but were always bigger than life. In all the scenes of this play, Henry must dominate; he may seem to be led by Wolsey, by Cromwell, seem to give in to Anne Boleyn and other wives, but, in the end, he dominates. Marquis sees Henry VIII as a sincere Catholic who doesn't find Roman Catholicism enough; on the other hand, he is a realist who will do whatever is necessary to strengthen England and to give him an heir. It would be very difficult to treat Henry VIII as a tragic hero; Marquis makes no attempt to do so. There is no attempt to explain the inconsistencies in the King's character. They are what make him memorable. He could, on the same day, compose a poem, condemn a man to death, woo a new wife, and plan complex strategy against France or Spain, depending on who the enemy was at that moment.

While *Master of the Revels,* on the whole, does not demonstrate a great dramatic talent, it has passages that show Marquis's ability as a humorist. At the beginning of Act Two, the King is suffering from gout while watching his armies marching off to fight Spain. At the same time, with the help of Sir Thomas More, he is writing a theological work which he hopes will please the Pope enough to grant the King a divorce from Catherine of Aragon:

HENRY [dictating to More]
  Say in my book that the Church is my Mother. . . .
  Say in my book that I am the obedient son of the Church. His Holiness will like that, won't he?
WOLSEY and MORE [together]
  He will, Your Highness.
HENRY
  Say in my book that this pestilential Martin Luther, this renegade monk, this arch-heretic, is an enemy of God!
  [A spasm of gout; then with vehemence:]
  This Martin Luther is a lousy, whoreson knave!
  [He identifies Luther with the pain in his foot.]
  This Luther is a scald-pated, bastardly, pernicious, evil-living, hypocritical scoundrel! Put that in good Latin, Sir Thomas.[13]

The humor here is quite obvious, but it works. It makes Henry VIII bigger than life, a figure who would dominate any society. In fact, the King insists on this point during the last scene. With his court, he is waiting for the cannon to fire, a sign that Catherine Howard has been executed:

HENRY
    I've always wanted something . . . and I don't know what it is. I've had women . . . and power . . . and . . . everything I wanted . . . and when I got it, I didn't want it . . . but I've missed . . . I don't know . . . It is something else I wanted!
    [Reflecting:]
    . . . I would always have had power. I mean if I'd been born a butcher's son, like Wolsey, I'd have got my hands on it, somehow . . . I'd have climbed to power . . . fought my way to it! I'm that kind of a man, Tom.[14]

This does not make Henry VIII a tragic figure. He is frustrated, not certain that his power has made him happy; yet, a moment or two later, he is holding Catherine Parr on his knee and kissing her as the cannon fires. The play ends with the King calling for music and wine; the dancers take over the stage.

Marquis does have some success with the other characters. Anne Boleyn is sexually aggressive; Sir Thomas More is properly heroic. Yet, there is not much in *Master of the Revels* that would indicate Marquis is a better-than-average playwright. In comparison with his other plays about the past, *Master of the Revels* is more conventional than either *The Dark Hours* or *Out of the Sea*. True, Marquis does invent speeches and does ignore strict historical accuracy; however, his characterization of Henry VIII and his court is exactly what the general public would expect, based on what little they would know.

Some of Marquis's best friends, and possibly Marquis himself, believed that, if he had received more encouragement and better productions, he could have become one of the leading American dramatists. The evidence for this belief is dubious. Had Marquis stuck to writing melodramatic comedies like *The Old Soak,* he might well have become as successful a playwright as George Ade. Today, a repertory company could do worse than staging a revival of *Out of the Sea*, or, even possibly, *The Dark Hours*. In all fairness, however, if Don Marquis is ever recognized as being much more than the creator of Archy and Mehitabel, it will not be because of his plays.

CHAPTER 9

"The Damnedest Book"[1]: Marquis's Unclassifiable Humor

W HILE much of Marquis's successful humorous writing fits recognizable literary genres, there are a few works which, while quite successful as humor, resist such classification. This should not be surprising since, like other columnists, Marquis collected his columns in various books that often had little over all organization. Two works, both drawn from his columns, particularly stand out as unclassifiable and highly successful: *Prefaces* (1919) and *The Almost Perfect State* (1927). Each allows Marquis to use his comic talent freely; each one still retains a good deal of its comic effectiveness.

I Prefaces

As the title suggests, *Prefaces* is a collection of introductions to thirty-two imaginary works, including a calendar, a book of safety pins, a checkbook, a memorandum book, a miser's autobiography, *Old Doctor Gumph's Almanac,* a moral book on arithmetic, a hangman's diary, a book of fishhooks, and a cookbook.[2]

In his affectionate essay about Marquis, Bernard DeVoto tells of trying to buy a copy of *Prefaces* in Chicago in 1919. The bookstore clerk thought DeVoto wanted H. L. Mencken's *A Book of Prefaces,* but DeVoto was finally able to get the book he wanted. He found that it made the Chicago–New York railroad trip " . . . smoother than I find it these days."[3]

Another contemporary of Marquis's referred to *Prefaces* as " . . . a book of whimsical essays."[4] Although usually associated with children's books, "whimsey" does suggest the rather playful, exaggerated nature of *Prefaces.* In almost every preface, Marquis uses the work being prefaced as a jumping off point for a comic excursion, allowing him to

118 DON MARQUIS

gently satirize human behavior and to parody various types of popular
literature.

The first preface, Marquis's personal favorite (Anthony, 205), "Preface to a Book of Literary Reminiscences" is a clever, mildly biting parody of a type of literature still popular today: a glorification of the past
at the expense of the present. The preface begins with a lament:

> They are tearing the old chop house down—the Eheu Fugaces chop
> house—to build on its site a commercial enterprise, a sordid publishing house.
> . . . So passes another literary landmark; mere business triumphs again over
> the Arts. (3)

Besides the obvious downgrading of publishing companies, Marquis
establishes the nostalgic, sentimental "I was there and saw all of the
famous people" tone that makes such literary reminiscences a success.

The rest of this preface is a series of anecdotes using famous literary
figures of the past, ranging from "Mike" Cervantes to "Jolly Jack"
Whittier, "Roaring Hank" Longfellow, and "Ollie" Holmes. In some
ways, the preface is similar to Twain's Whittier Birthday Speech which
portrayed Longfellow, Holmes, and Emerson as ne'er-do-well frontier
figures. While referring to numerous "sacred" American and Euro-
pean figures in such familiar terms, Marquis gets additional humor
from the belief that anything a celebrity does or says is witty and memorable. This is obvious from our first view of the chop house:

> It was in 1850 that Jack Whittier first brought me in to dinner there. Jolly
> Jack Whittier! There was a wit and a true Bohemian for you! His quickness
> at repartee was marvelous. Mike Cervantes was drinking in the bar as we
> passed through.
> "Hello, Jack," hiccoughed Mike, "been snowbounding lately?"
> "No," said Whittier, with a sidelong look at Mike's glass, "nor skating
> either."
> "Ralphie Emerson has more humor," Ollie Holmes used to say, "but, after
> all, Whittier is wittier!" (3–4)

Since Marquis is dealing with the dead, not speaking to friends and
admirers of the writers mentioned, he runs little danger of being crit-
icized. Also, Marquis is more concerned with satirizing the sort of false
nostalgia he would have found at the Players Club and in various New
York literary and journalistic circles.

Walt Whitman, who was a frequenter of the old chop house, is also the subject of a paragraph in "Preface to the Prospectus of a Club":

> Walt Whitman used to live over there (Brooklyn) and edit the *Eagle* and go swimming in Buttermilk Channel, two points off the starboard bow of Hank Beecher's church. Once an old Long Island skipper sunk a harpoon into Walt's haunch when he came up to blow, and the poet, snorting and bellowing and spouting verse, towed the whaler and his vessel clear out to Montauk before he shook the iron loose. Is there a bard in Greenwich Village that could do that? Not even Jack Reed, who writes like Byron and swims like Leander, could do that. (64)

In referring to this paragraph, Christopher Morley insisted that " . . . this casual comic paragraph, in the very guts and gusto of its Munchausenism, contains more shrewd criticism . . . than many a whole serious tome about Moby Walt."[5] Morley is asking the paragraph to carry too much critical weight; however, its comic success is undeniable. Purely as a tall tale, the view of Whitman is a throwback to Davy Crockett and the half-horse, half-alligator figures of the old Southwest. It also invokes the same nostalgia for a past when poets were truly heroic.

When Marquis turned to more current topics, he became more biting in his humor. In another preface, "Foreword to a Censor's Autobiography," Marquis satirizes Puritanism from the viewpoint of H. L. Mencken and the Jazz Age. Since Marquis composed unpublishable limericks and wrote ribald letters treasured by his friends, he would have welcomed this change to ridicule prudery.

In the "Foreword," Marquis has the censor pride himself on having " . . . a sixth sense which directs me infallibly to the detection of obscenity" (234). No author is safe from this sixth sense:

> Authors may talk of art, and chatter of its relation to life—they may prattle of truth and duty—but they cannot hide from me the carnal thought and the lascivious intention behind their specious innocence!
>
> A thing is either pure or it is impure. My sixth sense informs me at once. No argument is necessary. My spirit is either shocked or it is not shocked.
>
> It is not necessary to understand art in order to condemn it.
>
> I love to sit in my library with the hundreds of books and pictures I have condemned about me and think that I have been of some use to my generation. In my mind's eye, as I run my physical eye over the book bindings, I

can see the improper passages quivering and glowing inside the volumes . . .
I tremble, and at times my eyes fill with tears, as I repeat them aloud. (235–
36)

The implication that the censor gets sensual satisfaction from even
thinking of the improper passages, in addition to the demotion of art
to a moral cause, makes the censor ridiculous and somewhat pathetic.

Finally, in "Preface to the Plays of Euripides," Marquis displays a
variety of humorous talents. Like many other American humorists, he
begins the preface by making himself look ridiculous:

We were fussing around the office of the Atlanta (Ga.) *Journal* one morning about three o'clock, having just finished writing an editorial which we
thought would likely elect Hoke Smith governor, if he were able to live up
to it, when we ran across a copy of "Iphigenia in Tauris." . . . We happened
to know the alphabet and could mispronounce a few words, and we turned
over the pages wishing that we were able to read the thing—it might give us
a chance to elevate our mind, which was suffering from the frightful strain
of writing about Hoke Smith in such a way that even Hoke would believe
himself a statesman. And thinking about how great a man Euripides probably
was, for all we knew, and how superior to Hoke Smith he must have been in
many ways, we got hungry. (47–48)

Besides his own ridiculousness, making Hoke Smith (an ex-member
of Cleveland's cabinet who became governor of Georgia and later a
senator from that state) or any politician believe he is a statesman is a
tall tale in the tradition of native American humor. The effort of taking
a politician seriously leads Marquis to a Greek lunchroom across the
street from the newspaper office.

While Marquis is discussing the plays of Euripides with the owner
of the lunchroom, another customer, a young man named Henry, has
what appears to be a heart attack. Thinking quickly, Marquis orders
the proprietor to apply hot hamburger steaks to Henry's chest. When
Henry asks Marquis to pray for him, Marquis begins to chant one of
the choruses from Euripides which uses the word "Basileon." After
Marquis repeats the word "Basileon" eighteen times, the lunchroom
owner announces that he has run out of hamburger steaks. Marquis
advises him to switch to fried eggs. When a doctor finally arrives, he
compliments Marquis for using heat; however, Henry insists he was
saved by the prayer. Then, in true deadpan fashion, Marquis drops in
a paragraph of seemingly serious literary criticism comparing Euri-

pides with Aeschylus and Sophocles—almost as if he must get the preface back on the right track and somehow end it. His concluding sentence links three dissimilar people: "Henry married, Hoke Smith in the Senate, Euripides dead—how time flies!" (53). Thus, he makes all three seem insignificant, which is probably what he had in mind all along.

In *Prefaces*, Marquis was able to use his humorous talents fully: burlesque, satire, storytelling, tall tales, all work well together. Certainly, all of the prefaces are not humorous masterpieces. Yet, *Prefaces* is a neglected work, showing that Marquis could write the humorous "pieces" so prized by Thurber, Benchley, and others.

II   The Almost Perfect State

Much more obviously than in *Prefaces*, Marquis also drew on his columns for *The Almost Perfect State* (1927).[6] Because of this the book might be called a notebook for a utopia since it is not very coherent or organized. As Marquis himself admits in the introduction, this book is made up of columns from "The Sun Dial" and "The Lantern" which are reprinted just as they were written:

> What they were when they came hot and hasty from the typewriter, that they still are; and they can be made into nothing else. They are full of repetitions of ideas, and even of phraseology; and they reveal that the writer never seemed to be able to make up his mind, from one day to another, just how seriously he wanted them to be taken. (4)

Besides the accuracy of Marquis's own criticism, his evaluation again shows his desire to be taken seriously; yet, as he suggests in the book itself, he also knows that it isn't healthy for a human being to be taken too seriously.

Critical response to *The Almost Perfect State* has been generally favorable; however, Christopher Morley insists that although *The Almost Perfect State* and *Chapters for the Orthodox* " ... most clearly represent the moody and shifting interchange of his [Marquis's] thinking," they "... proved to be almost completely unsalable."[7] A recent critic uses Marquis's own words to dismiss the book, believing that the book offers, "limited satisfaction" as a " ... half-serious, half-whimsical melange of utopian philosophical observations and personal prejudices."[8] While Bernard DeVoto agrees that the book is exasperating, he admires it for these very qualities: "It is the damnedest book but which of Don's books isn't?"[9] Will Cuppy, another popular humorist, liked Marquis's utopia because it is " . . . probably the only one fit to live in" (Anthony, 428). The most serious evaluation of *The Almost Perfect State* is in Norris Yates's chapter on Marquis in his study of modern American humor. Yates sees the book as dealing with " . . . man's need to live in harmony with his nonhuman surroundings."[10] Yates places heavy emphasis on Marquis's agrarianism, linking him with Jefferson's views of the city. In Marquis's " . . . longing for a simple agrarian society purged of commercialism and prudery," he "exemplified a major literary tradition that included, despite their differences, Thoreau, John Burroughs, Mark Twain, Robert Frost, William Faulkner, E. B. White. . . ."[11] Yates also sees Marquis as being essentially pessimistic since his ideal society has been lost; in fact, in Yates's view, Marquis is a naturalist who sees man as " . . . hopelessly separated from nature."[12] There is really no way to remedy the situation except to wait for something better to evolve: "He [Marquis] made it clear that in *The Almost Perfect State* he was just getting his kicks through utopian speculation."[13]

In *The Almost Perfect State* Marquis firmly believes that if opportunities for fun are available, everything else will fall into place. Very early he makes this clear when replying to the query of what the inhabitants of his state will do with all the leisure time they will enjoy because of a more simplified, less industrialized society:

> They will tell stories and listen to stories; they will run foot races with one another; they will write plays and act them and no one will get rich from it; they will go swimming and drink enough to be happy without becoming sots; they will go fishing oftener; they will speculate on man's destiny and cultivate their religious natures and go to chicken fights and ball games and discover new gods and sit in the shade and smoke; they will eat excellent food without becoming gluttons, and make love without becoming jealous; they will invent new arts and new games and new duties, and everyone will live five hundred years and be glad of it and never have the toothache; they will pitch horseshoes and write poems and build beautiful buildings and recite limericks to one another. (17–18)

This is not a society Thoreau would feel completely comfortable in, but Twain and Faulkner would certainly feel at home. Certainly, one must take Marquis's description as somewhat tongue-in-cheek, but note that, underneath the heavy emphasis on simply enjoying life, there is the strong implication that the individual will lead a more creative life—even when he becomes old.

In fact, possibly the most controversial premise put forward by Marquis in the entire book is that "The Almost Perfect State will not be governed by businessmen, but by artists" (47). Artists will lead because they " . . . know more than anything else about play, which is art, which is creation . . . the people of this earth must listen to their artists; must make them their guides and governors in all things, must come to realize that to give heed to anyone but the artists upon any subject whatever is damned nonsense . . ." (50). Interestingly, Marquis insists that a world which is governed by artists will have to be made up of a new species. Yet, throughout history, individuals prophetic of this new species have appeared: Socrates, Buddha, Moses, Jesus, Emerson (37). Like Thoreau, Marquis believed that the perfect state is possible only when inhabited by individuals who are capable of self-government, without any formal governmental structure such as we have today:

> Perhaps some day there will be a community in which nearly all of the individuals will be capable of self government, and then they will govern themselves; they will have a pure democracy. . . . (74)

Until this happens, the majority should be ruled by a genuine aristocracy with the qualities of Jesus and Lincoln. Here, as in other parts of his utopia, Marquis is reflecting the views of Jefferson who, in a famous letter to John Adams, agreed that " . . . there is a natural aristocracy among men. The grounds of this are virtue and talent."[14] After distinguishing between this natural aristocracy and what Jefferson calls an "artificial" aristocracy " . . . founded on wealth and birth, without either virtue or talents . . ." Jefferson insists " . . . that form of government is best which provides the most effectually for a pure selection of these natural *aristoi* into the offices of government[.]"[15] Unlike Marquis, Jefferson did not see the possibility of a step beyond this form of government. He believed that in a free election, educated citizens could elect " . . . the really good and wise."[16] Marquis, writing one hundred years later, would be more pessimistic, having seen the American voters pick such natural aristocrats as Warren Harding.

Marquis's views are also Jeffersonian in regard to education and man's relationship with nature. In regard to education, Jefferson believed in an educated electorate who would pick the best man—the "natural aristocrat"—to govern. Marquis also saw education as a key to his state being realized. However, he largely rejected formal education as practiced in the United States:

> ... The desire of Eminent Educators ... is to train up a nation patterned intellectually in the mold of the Eminent Educators. They are perpetually defeated by the resisting power of the popular intellect and instinct. (65)

Certainly, Emerson and Thoreau would applaud this view, which is not so much antiintellectual as it is proindividual. The only way for an individual to be educated in the truth is to create a new system of education which would " ... make all men aware that they are gods in the making and that they can walk upon the water if they will" (70). If one did not know better, he might try to find this passage in *Walden* or in one of Emerson's essays. Marquis doesn't offer any very specific organization for his type of education; however, as in other parts of the book, he plays down the seriousness of his proposals by inviting those who don't like his theory of education to make their own theory.

Much closer to Jefferson's agrarianism is Marquis's view of man's relationship with his environment. From the beginning of *The Almost Perfect State*, it is clear that Marquis believes man has lost whatever relationship he once had with nature. While Marquis doesn't see much chance of this relationship returning, unless over a very long period of time, he does have a vision of what an almost perfect relationship between man and nature would be like. One key requirement is less people: "Our perfect state will not be thickly populated; there should be about ten millions of people scattered over an area equal to that of the United States" (6). Specifically, the population of the entire world should be kept " ... well under a hundred million" (10). This reduction in population will accomplish several things; first, it will bring happiness: "The way for the world to secure a larger share of happiness for its children is to have fewer children. Then each child will have more happiness" (6). Second, it will do away with large cities:

> Such enormous congregations of people as New York and London and Chicago with their slums and their false riches and their ugly ostentation and real misery and sham magnificence, are as anamolous on the face of the earth ... as warts and blackheads on an angel's nose. (11)

Third, it will restore man's original relationship with nature:

> The greater part of the globe would return to wilderness and be reinhabited by wild animals in vast numbers, so that those who fancied it might always go forth and live much as the North American Indians did, returning to the cultivated districts when they tired of being nomads. (10–11)

It is rather comic, in itself, that a man who spent nearly all of his adult life living and working in large cities takes much the same view of them as Jefferson who believed that "the mobs of great cities add just so much to the support of pure government as sores do to the strength of the human body."[17] Also, like Jefferson, Marquis saw his state having only what little business and industry was absolutely necessary. This would make the world less complicated and would do away with a good deal of the strife now plaguing the world.

When Marquis looks at the present, he sees no sign that this happy, natural state is conceivable. In the bitterest part of the book, he lashes out at the way man has treated nature:

> The pig that lies in his own trough wastes half of his own swill. Greed is always stupid. The wanton destruction of the national resources in this country must be paid for not only by this generation but by the next one and the next one after that.
>
> . . . Let a tribe cheat the earth—coin its rainfall and its heat and its wind into dollars, beyond present need and reason, use up within this decade all the nitrates the soil was putting away in a savings bank for future generations, always taking and giving nothing in return, always reaping and never sowing—and the earth will take a vengeance on that tribe, choke the streams and overlay the valleys with sand and then sulk for a century or so in sullen infertility. (53)

If Marquis sees no very clear solution, today it is quite clear that what Marquis said in 1927 could take place in the last quarter of the twentieth century.

The only concrete proposal offered to forestall this grim future is that "in the Almost Perfect State no man shall be allowed to cut down a tree unless he plants at least two" (52). While this may be feasible, when put against the vastness of the problem, it offers little more than a finger in the dike. The key to Marquis's view may be simply, as Yates suggests, his yearning " . . . for the small towns and green fields of his boyhood. . . ."[18]

It is impossible to resolve the book's contradictions into a total, rational, philosophical vision of an ideal world. The very format of the book argues against taking it too seriously or making it the subject of a ponderous analysis. Each chapter follows a similar format, mixing serious thoughts with comic relief. In the midst of a discussion of the need for diversity in the Almost Perfect State, certainly a serious-sounding topic, Marquis insists that citizens of the Almost Perfect State will be sparsely dressed. He follows this with a "Declaration": "You may clothe part of the people all of the time or all of the people part of the time, but you cannot force all the people to wear all their clothes all the time" (43).

The key to appreciating *The Almost Perfect State* is to realize that it is designed for Clem Hawley and not for Henry David Thoreau. It is a state where Clem and his beloved old-time "patreeyarch" could live idyllically. It is a paradise very similar to the paradise pictured in Elmer Rice's popular comedy *The Adding Machine*. Mr. Zero, the "hero" of *The Adding Machine*, rejects this paradise, as described by another character in the play, preferring to spend his time working a gigantic adding machine:

They [the people in Rice's paradise such as Swift and Rabelais] seem to think of nothing but enjoyment or of wasting their time in profitless occupations. Some paint pictures from morning until night, or carve blocks of stone. Others write songs or put words together, day in and day out. Still others do nothing but lie under the trees and look at the sky. There are men who spend all their time reading books and women who think only of adorning themselves. And forever they are telling stories and laughing and singing and drinking and dancing. There are drunkards, thieves, vagabonds, blasphemers, adulterers.[19]

Many Americans would find it hard to accept a state where work was a vice and pleasure was a virtue. In reading *The Almost Perfect State* today, one should regard it as the paradise of a man who believed in not taking life too seriously, but who could also believe that life's highest purpose was to create.

CHAPTER 10

Marquis and God:
"The Divinity Student"

I *"The God-Maker Man"*

ANYONE who has read even a few of Don Marquis's works would recognize the appropriateness of Christopher Morley's reference to Marquis as a " . . . divinity student."[1] Throughout his work, Marquis uses not only the Bible for literary purposes, but the whole concept of belief, the struggle between the body and the spirit. At his most obvious, he has The Old Soak give his versions of well-known Old Testament episodes. The Old Soak is quite orthodox in his beliefs, expressing a deep dislike for that "damned little athyiss" Hennery Withers. When Withers makes fun of the story of Jonah, The Old Soak becomes indignant: "Only its friends got a right to laugh at that story."[2] To Clem Hawley and to Marquis, "orthodox" did not mean the grim, repressive fundamentalism Marquis pictures in *Sons of the Puritans*. An acceptance of Christ did not mean an acceptance of the brand of Christianity decreed by any one church or society.

During his lifetime, some acquaintances claimed that Marquis did become a Christian Scientist to please Marjorie Marquis. Marquis may have been a Christian Scientist briefly. In an unpublished chapter of his egobiography, he claimed that the only two Christian denominations he could ever connect himself with were the Roman Catholics and Christian Scientists. Typically, he rejected the Roman Catholic Church because he felt squeamish when he thought of actual blood and flesh being drunk and eaten during the Mass. He also rejected Christian Science for aesthetic reasons, largely the poor quality of Mrs. Eddy's poetry. (Anthony, 419). Marquis also disliked Mrs. Eddy's ban on liquor, tobacco, tea, or coffee; however, he believed many Christian Scientists didn't take these bans seriously.

Marquis's objections to Catholicism and Christian Science should be taken, as they are intended, as tongue-in-cheek jibes. Yet, even though he rejected most organized religious groups, he did have a clear set of beliefs which are expressed in his writing. At the center of Marquis's faith was the creative force of the human spirit. Whether or not this makes him a Platonist, it is a particularly useful belief for an artist because there is no place for fear in this faith. In "Preface to the Works of Billy Sunday," Marquis scorns the heavy emphasis on fear of Hell in Sunday's preachings. It is not proof of a creed to have someone accept it because of fear. Man must be inspired, must be given something to work toward, not merely be promised that if one is good, he won't be punished. A reliance on Hell to make people believe is a reversal to " . . . the silly tales we gibbered when we were blue-lipped apes back yonder in the gray dawn of time; and one day it will fall on silence; there will come a language in which the thing [Hell] is not. As skulls grow broader, so do creeds."[3]

In one of his best-known poems, "The God-Maker Man," Marquis traces man's god-making from ancient Greece and the Orient to the present; however, he does not see present gods as being superior to ancient gods:

> For no form of a god and no fashion
> Man has made in his desperate passion
> But is worthy some worship of mine;—
> Not too hot with a gross belief,
> Nor yet too cold with pride,
> I will bow me down where my brothers bow,
> Humble—but open-eyed![4]

Man creates the gods he needs. What Marquis objects to in much of his writing is the narrowminded intolerance of any god except one's own personal god. One must be "open-eyed," always ready to question, to expose fraudulent beliefs, but one must also always be humble before another's sincere beliefs.

Marquis's belief in the dominance of the spiritual side of man—the creative force of the universe as Marquis saw it—is undoubtedly what made him inhabit the Almost Perfect State with artists. In similar fashion when asked by *American Magazine* to respond to a letter asking for proof of life after death, Marquis's conclusion was that there is no real proof, that most people take belief for proof. In the last part of this article, after admitting that he has gone through periods of belief and disbelief over eternal life, Marquis debates what form life after death will take. He is certain that the mind, spirit, or soul (he uses all three terms) will survive the death of the body since the spirit is made up of the same "stuff" as the "central and animating spirit of the universe."[5] Although Marquis did not write seriously about this question at any great length, it is clear that his sarcastic treatment of transmigration of souls in *Archy and Mehitabel* is directed more at the hokum he always found as a part of any fad or belief. Marquis's own view of the evolution of man's spirit—the permanence of man's creativity—was unchangeable.

Although Marquis used his beliefs throughout his career, two separate events in the early 1930s, both having negative economic effects on his career, were the culmination of these beliefs. In 1932, *The Dark Hours* failed on Broadway; in 1934, *Chapters for the Orthodox* failed to attract a very large audience, although it received generally favorable reviews. Marquis had counted on *The Dark Hours* to solve his acute financial problems. After its failure, he would certainly have had even higher hopes for *Chapters for the Orthodox*.

II Chapters for the Orthodox

As shown in an earlier chapter, *The Dark Hours* is an orthodox treatment of Christ's trial and crucifixion. *Chapters for the Orthodox*, despite its title, is more original. The specific idea behind *Chapters for the Orthodox* comes from Marquis's sympathy with the feeling that God and Satan exist as beings who participate personally in man's destiny:

... it occurred to me to write a book in which Jehovah and Satan should go about New York City today and do much the same sort of thing that they are reported to have done some centuries ago on another portion of this queer little planet's surface.[6]

Of the twelve chapters in *Chapters for the Orthodox*, most fit Marquis's description of the book. A few do not. He reprinted one story, "The Other Room," as "The Case of the Eminent Neurologist," adding only a new name and a brief introduction which ties the story into the basic structure of the book. Two other chapters, "Old Man Murtrie"

and "The Devil, the Flea, and the Millenium," were first published in
earlier collections. Nearly all of the chapters deal, in one way or
another, with Jehovah, Christ, and the Devil in New York City. Besides
this rather loose unity of theme, approximately half the chapters use
the character of Twiller Van Durden, a painter who becomes
acquainted with Christ. When read today, these accounts do not seem
shocking. Many of them are based on the "what if" formula; that is,
what if God were walking on earth? What if Christ came again?
Would he be crucified? What if God decided on another Virgin Birth
to save New York City?

For the most part, the people of New York are no more willing to
accept Christ, to please God or to resist the Devil than people of other
civilizations have been. In the opening chapter, "Miss Higginbotham
Declines," Jehovah is not sure what to do with New York. He doesn't
want to destroy it although some evangelists are insisting that this will
happen. Even the idea of a second flood doesn't appeal to Him since
He no longer cares for violent physical force. He also rejects destroying
New York because people are no longer so adamant in their demands
for the total destruction of their enemies, "—the extreme religionists,
and the more fervid patriots, of course, always excepted, and the
professional warriors" (CFO, 6).

Jehovah is then inspired to send another Begotten Son. The first one
worked better than anything else Jehovah has tried to improve human
conduct. He next decides that the second Begotten Son should also be
born of a virgin: "They had had a Begotten Son born of a virgin; and
if they got another Begotten Son, and he *wasn't* born of a virgin, as
like as not they wouldn't think he was really a Begotten Son at all"
(CFO, 8).

After making his decision, Jehovah acts. He goes to Miss Higginbotham's home to tell her of the great honor she is being given. Miss
Higginbotham's ancestors came over on the *Mayflower* and she is
determined to remain a Puritan in the face of the general moral
decline in New York. Thus, when Jehovah, whom she recognizes
instantly, informs her that she is being given a great honor, Miss Higginbotham is insulted and disappointed. She rejects the idea of bearing
a child out of wedlock even if the child would bring happiness to millions of people. When Jehovah offers to marry Miss Higginbotham, she
refuses because she does not approve of polygamy. If, on the other
hand, Jehovah was not married to the mother of His first son, Miss

Higginbotham could not associate with Him, either. When Jehovah, now becoming irritated, asks her if it is true she does not approve of the former Virgin Birth, her reply is unorthodox: "It was all right for those times . . . but I do hope we have made some progress morally in the last 1900 years!" (CFO, 20).

Jehovah knows that Miss Higginbotham will expect Him to respect her motives; her God would do so. Also, He is not now so convinced that she would be the ideal mother for the new savior. Nevertheless, Jehovah's mission is not in vain. The maid, a common but quite attractive young woman, thinks Jehovah is sexually attractive. Realizing this, Jehovah " . . . turned and gazed upon her from the doorstep, long and smilingly, and an ecstatic thrill pervaded the vital creature. Within a year she gave birth to a son, and this child may be somewhere in the world now, and it is possible that great, saintly things are to be expected of him" (CFO, 21).

This chapter is fairly typical of the other chapters. Marquis takes one of the central events in Christianity and insists upon its viability, even in the modern world. Miss Higginbotham is the unorthodox Christian who cannot accept Jehovah's actions, substituting her moral standards, or, as Twain might call it, her "moral sense." Of course, Marquis, as he admitted in the preface, is hitting at hypocrisy—a target he would also belabour in *The Sons of the Puritans*. By making Jehovah a gentleman who refuses to force himself or his power on those who cannot or will not believe, Marquis modernizes God; He is the Jehovah upper-class New York would expect—if not always accept.

Besides Jehovah's spending time in New York, Jesus is also fond of making appearances in the city. We first see him at the beginning of Chapter 3, sitting on a bench in Central Park. When he repairs a little girl's broken doll by passing his walking stick over the pieces, Twiller Van Durden, who, when not in his artist's shack on Long Island, spends time in conventional settings, is sitting nearby, introduces himself. When Twiller questions Jesus about miracles, Jesus admits that miracles often get in the way of his ideas: "People hate to think! I would have quit miracles altogether but for the fact that there were so many sick and mentally deranged persons always about" (CFO, 37).

After a lengthy discussion, Twiller leaves to attend a dinner at the home of his brother, Walter, a wealthy banker whose wife is a social climber. As Twiller arrives at the dinner, he is still full of the inspiration he received from Jesus. Particularly, he believes he has been too

harsh in his judgment of people; he must be more forgiving. The chapter reaches its climax at the dinner party. At the close of the dinner, as the women are leaving, Twiller gets to his feet and announces that everyone should forgive his sister-in-law. When Mrs. Van Durden asks for what should she be forgiven, Twiller's reply is simple:

"Why," said he, "you know—for your adulteries."
He added, without any perception whatever of the devastating effect of his words: "Like Jesus, you know! He forgave the adultress!" (CFO, 52)

The conclusion doesn't quite fit the chapter. However, it does confirm the difficulty of following Christ while conforming to social conventions. It is not entirely clear why Twiller could not have forgiven his sister-in-law privately. Evidently, Marquis wants the reader to believe that, at this point, Twiller has identified totally with Jesus.

Twiller identifies even more emphatically with Jesus in "Twiller Van Durden's Miracle." As mentioned previously, Jesus did not place miracles very high on his list of priorities. In the letter to Morley, Marquis insists that he does not believe in miracles. Yet, in a letter to Hugh Walpole, Marquis also insists that it is very difficult to get an accurate picture of Jesus through the Gospels. For instance, Marquis refuses to believe that Jesus ever made any threat regarding hellfire and eternal damnation. Such threats would be entirely inconsistent with his teaching love and brotherhood. Correspondingly, when Twiller Van Durden questions Jesus about the miracle of the fig tree, in which Christ supposedly cursed a fig tree so that it withered and died, he can't even remember the miracle. After reading the biblical account, he can't understand how it was ever included. However, Jesus is not worried that false stories about him have gotten into the Gospels, since they also contain his basic ideas.

Before Twiller has a chance to explore these ideas fully with Christ, he is arrested at an Italian restaurant where Jesus, at Twiller's urging, changed water into wine to accommodate a wedding party. Jesus is charged with being a bootlegger, anarchist, blasphemer, and atheist by those present, without any proof being offered.

After being arrested, Christ is brought before a group of leading citizens meeting in a newly constructed church. They are worried about Jesus, whom they refer to as "Josephson," because he has been spreading dangerous ethical ideas. A tremendous argument develops over where Jesus came from and what his beliefs are:

A well-known radical, who was frequently described as a Philosophical Anarchist, got up and denied that Jesus was an anarchist. . . . In the following two minutes he was also repudiated by a Communist, a Socialist, a Bolshevist sympathizer, a Holy Roller, a Theosophist, an International Banker, a Prohibitionist, and a Vegetarian. (CFO, 146)

After these repudiations, the few Jewish rabbis in attendance leave, claiming that, once again, the whole Jewish people are going to be blamed for the actions of a few influential citizens. After more angry accusations, a newspaper editor declares that they want to get rid of Christ because they can't exist in a society that practices Christ's ideals. They must be prepared either to follow Christ's teachings or eliminate him.

When the leading citizens cannot decide what to do with Christ, he goes to the nave of the church, where he crucifies himself by changing places with a statue of Christ. Ever afterwards, this statue of Christ appears to have a faintly satirical smile, possibly " . . . having something to do with the fact that the eyes of the statue are fixed all day long upon the golden legend at the opposite end of the church: THE GREATEST OF THESE IS CHARITY" (CFO, 157).

Twiller Van Durden's own miracle occurs the summer after Christ's second crucifixion. He is terrified by the thought that people may discover he is able, simply by wishing, to make a figure of mud and sticks, created by children, fly. Unfortunately, Friday, an American Indian with some black blood, has seen the miracle. He insists that Twiller make him white. Twiller refuses, giving Friday some clothing instead. Twiller then finds himself performing miracles against his better judgment. Even when Twiller prays to have this power taken from him so that he will be able to live like other men, his prayer is unanswered. Finally, Twiller is confronted by the corpse of Friday who has been killed in an accident. Without meaning to, he raises Friday from the dead and flees in horror. Suddenly, he finds himself, with Christ, walking across the Atlantic; Friday is following them, with some difficulty. Jesus insists that Friday is alive only because Twiller thinks so. Faced with the possibility of having Friday, dead or alive, following him forever, Twiller decides to perform one final experiment by sinking beneath the waves to see if there is life after death:

Friday . . . we've both got to the place where there's very little more in it, for either one of us, on the physical plane of existence. You sink, and I will,

too; and a couple of minutes afterwards we'll know whether there is anything or not in all this stuff about the spirit living on after the death of the body. (CFO, 202)

Twiller's suicide leaves the question of miracles unresolved. What Marquis suggests is that the ability to perform miracles would not necessarily be a blessing. In comparison to Little Satan in *The Mysterious Stranger*, who performs tricks involving the death of innocent people, Twiller's power, and, by implication, Christ's power, will not allow him to be so impersonal. Yet, as Twiller senses while sinking, possibly the whole thing is nothing more than magic, having little or nothing to do with Christ's central significance.

Although it may not be apparent from what has been said so far, there is a good deal of humor in *Chapters for the Orthodox*. Much of the humor comes from Marquis's literalness, his taking Jehovah, Jesus, and Satan pretty much as they are described and the events around these figures pretty much as they supposedly occurred. However, in three of the more successful chapters, he allows his imagination to operate more freely. Two of these chapters are in dramatic form and could, I believe, be performed today. The other is a very short story, showing Twain's influence. This story, "Satan Goes to Church," supposedly offended some ministers, stirring up a mild furor. Marquis sets the scene with deliberate simplicity:

Dr. David Bentley enjoyed a lucrative position as pastor of the church to which belonged one of the richest men in the world, Mr. Jefferson Pettigrew. One Sunday during the Lenten season, Mr. Pettigrew proceeded up the aisle arm in arm with no less a person than the Devil himself, and they sat down side by side in the Pettigrew pew.

Satan . . . had not even taken the trouble to disguise himself as an ordinary citizen, although he was considerate enough to hold his long spiked tail in such a position that it would not catch and snag the clothing of any of the other members of the congregation. He listened to the sermon in a decorous manner, and when the services were over lingered with Mr. Pettigrew to shake Dr. Bentley by the hand. (CFO, 53)

Ironically, although everyone present had recognized the Devil, no one would admit that he was present:

. . . it was not the Devil at all, but merely some eccentric friend of the great financier's. Some of them even claimed to know that he was a distant cousin of Mr. Pettigrew who was, unfortunately, a bit off mentally, and who persisted in putting on strange costumes and going about in them. (CFO, 53–54)

To this point, the story is mildly funny; then, Marquis quite calmly throws in a complication:

> Towards the end of the Service Satan nonchalantly . . . reached over into the pew in front of him and caught a young woman by the throat and strangled her to death. He was thirsty. He twisted her head off, quite calmly, and drank her blood, and threw the body into the aisle, and then picked up his hymn book and turned to the song which had just been announced, which he sang in a pleasing and sympathetic baritone.
> The young woman who belonged to a very good family, might have so far forgotten herself as to scream while she was being killed; but her mother's eye was on her, warning her . . . that it would never do to offend Mr. Pettigrew . . . she permitted herself to be strangled quietly, as a well-bred girl should. . . . Five newspaper reporters, who had also seen the Devil drink the blood, wrote it for their papers as an automobile accident, since the girl's family was of such prominence that something had to be said. (CFO, 54–55)

When Dr. Bentley confronts Mr. Pettigrew after the service, Pettigrew complains that the Devil insisted on coming to church, a request Pettigrew could not deny since "He's always intruding—in a business way you know" (CFO, 57). Bentley and Pettigrew agree that money is necessary for Christianity to operate successfully; in fact, Bentley insists that the money Pettigrew gives the church, " . . . was sanctified by the use to which it was put" (CFO, 58). The two agree that they will have to stand for the Devil attending church once a year around Easter for the good of the church. Marquis allows the Devil to have the last word: " 'I knew,' he said, 'that I wouldn't need to say anything. They always work around to the right point of view if you leave them to themselves'" (CFO, 59).

Marquis succeeds, in a few pages, in satirizing the link between materialism and a Christianity where Christ doesn't seem necessary. Throughout *Chapters for the Orthodox*, one feels that there is little room for Christ in today's church although there is room in Twiller Van Durden's shack on Long Island.

In the two dramatic chapters, the longest in the book, Marquis allows his imagination to range very freely. At the beginning of the first of these chapters, "Report of a Trial Which Was Not Printed," Twiller Van Durden accidentally wanders into a courtroom during a trial:

> Jesus of Nazareth was sitting, a somewhat puzzled prisoner, in front of a dais, on which sat no less a person than Jehovah himself, presiding as Judge. Jesus had been arraigned at the suit of a former Gadarean swine-breeder who charged Jesus with the wanton destruction of two thousand head of hogs,

which had rushed down a steep place into the sea and been drowned as a consequence of one of the Galilean prophet's most celebrated miracles. (CFO, 104)

Marquis was quite fond of the miracle of the Gadarean swine. He used it in the chapter during which Christ crucified himself. The swineherd was one of the witnesses in *The Dark Hours* and Marquis used the miracle in at least one magazine article.[7]

The jury foreman is G. B. Shaw. Other prominent jury members are St. Francis of Assisi, John Calvin, and Caiaphas. Satan is prosecuting the case and St. Paul acts as attorney for the defense. Obviously, in Marquis's mind, the prosecution has about as much chance of winning the case as Hamilton Burger ever had of convicting one of Perry Mason's clients.

During the course of the trial and in a brief conference in the Judge's chambers, Marquis manages to use many of the themes found elsewhere in *Chapters for the Orthodox*. For instance, the whole concept of miracles is brought under fire by Satan who attempts to show that Jesus acted malevolently toward the swineherd, the owner of the swine and the swine, themselves. St. Paul is able, on cross-examination, to satisfy the Judge, if not the reader, that the swineherd had a dubious character before the miracle, that the owner of the swine and his family were involved in numerous litigations and possessed dubious moral characters. As for the swine, since their destiny was to be killed, isn't it far more glorious to have died as the result of a divine act rather than in the slaughterhouse? At one point in the trial, G. B. Shaw causes general consternation in the court by insisting that Jehovah could, if he desired, abolish evil from the universe since he is all powerful. Both Satan and Paul object; Jehovah sustains the objection, adding that, from his view, the presence of both good and evil in the universe is not a contradiction.

During a break in the trial, Twiller Van Durden encounters Judas smoking a cigarette in the corridor. Here, Marquis is obviously looking back at *The Dark Hours*. When Twiller asks Judas why he betrayed Christ, Judas, again, insists that it was fate. God put evil in Judas's nature; Judas betrayed Christ to strike back at God. This reinforces the previously stated view of Jesus that he was crucified as a means of getting back at Jehovah. Also, when Judas claims that he wanted to use the thirty pieces of silver to retire and study theology, Marquis is again hitting a favorite target, one that would be safe since, to many people, theology is simply a way of over-intellectualizing beliefs.

The trial reaches a climax with Jesus on the stand being cross-examined by Satan. Jesus admits that he didn't feel sorry for the swine or for the swineherd who ended his life by being crucified as an outlaw. Satan is forced to apologize to the Judge when he states that it will be impossible to receive justice since the Judge is biased. Finally, he accuses Jesus of being a prophet. Jesus agrees, but defines "prophet" rather originally:

. . . a prophet is . . . a forerunner and example of a species which has not yet come into existence . . . Buddha was one of them; I was one of them; there have been many other individuals prophetic of the species to come. It is in this sense that I am a prophet. (CFO, 132–33)

This view, expressed by Marquis in *The Almost Perfect State*, is accepted by Jehovah since it doesn't conflict too much with predestination.

At this stage of the trial, St. Paul moves to have the case dismissed. Jehovah grants the motion, then says He wants to see Jesus and Paul in His chambers. As a representative of the press, Twiller Van Durden is allowed to be present. When in His chambers, Jehovah makes a lengthy statement about why it is bad to be a personal God instead of "Everything." The best thing is for a god not to explain anything:

Humanity may then learn to quit demanding personal gods and learn how to get contact with the spiritual substance of the universe without them. I am seriously contemplating abolishing myself as Jehovah and just melting back into Everything again. (CFO, 136)

Obviously, such a view fits Marquis's concept of mankind's spiritual evolution. The more sophisticated man becomes in his beliefs, the less he has need of a personal god. However, as with The Almost Perfect State, this stage of man's development will be a long time in arriving.

The conclusion of the trial is humorous. John Calvin is very upset because no one is to be beheaded. When Twiller asks Jehovah about predestination, Jehovah laughs, thinking of how Huck Finn called it "preforedestination." Twain used to worry about predestination, but he now spends most of his time conducting boat races on his river, ". . . with Mark on the deck of the winning ship, archangels, saints and devils lined up on the banks of the river shouting and cheering, the boats belching fire and smoke, and Mark making the welkin ring with profanity" (CFO, 138). Satan is very envious of Twain's river, but

Mark is unable to accept Satan's invitation to visit Hell with his river
for awhile. "His wife and William Dean Howells wouldn't let him.
They said it would look bad ... and Mark said if people didn't quit
editing him, he'd go to Hell and stay there" (CFO, 139). Jehovah then
explains that Hell was started by theologians to whom Jehovah had
given a tract of Heaven to live in as they pleased. Finally, Marquis
remarks that Twiller Van Durden wrote a story about the trial, but it
was never printed.

Besides the funny if rather obvious use of Twain and the interpretation of his life popular at that time, Marquis manages to treat some
very serious issues comically: free will, the existence of evil, and the
relationship between God and man. However, he still makes the reader
consider them on a more serious level while being humorous. Some
chapters of the book do this more successfully than others. The last
chapter, "A Moment in Hell," is a long one-act play which uses characters from *Faust* to elaborate on some serious issues. Faust sells his
soul to Mephisto in exchange for sexual potency. He meets Marguerite
and falls madly in love with her. Marguerite, pure and innocent, has
come to Hell hoping to comfort some of its inhabitants. Throughout
this chapter, the humor is rather obvious, but still manages to be generally effective. For instance, Mephisto's apartment is surrounded by
very high walls. At the top of these walls are deep windows at which
figures appear from time to time; when God is mentioned, "An
immense pink ear appears at one of the crenelations at the top of the
set, back" (CFO, 277). Mephisto then warns Faust that the walls have
ears. Throughout the chapter, a chorus of demons operates off stage,
making sarcastic comments.

The demons continue to make more and more sarcastic suggestions
about Faust until they are stopped by Mephisto, who then attempts to
convince Faust that the pleasures of the flesh are transitory; the flesh
is an illusion. Faust, with a violin playing in the background, replies
that he grew up idealizing women, seeing only the spiritual side, but,
at the age of forty, he was tempted by a female patient. Even though
he resisted her, she accused him, to her husband's face, of violating her
honor. At this point, Joseph laughs and his face appears at one of the
windows.

Since Faust is still a virgin, although very knowledgeable about
women, he wants to be young again. When Mephisto asks if there are
any particular women he would like as his mistresses, Faust suggests
Helen of Troy, Cleopatra, and Mae West. Mephisto asks one of his
aides where Mae West is. When he learns that she is in Hollywood, he

replies, "Tell her to drop whatever she has and come in. I've got a new contract for her" (CFO, 273). Mephisto warns Faust about the dangers of a good woman who insists on having a personal god for a lover. From offstage, Adam agrees with this.

As Faust prepares to drink the potion which will give him potency, Marguerite chases a few devils through Mephisto's apartment. Faust falls in love with her to the point of rejecting Helen of Troy, Catherine of Russia, Venus, Lucrezia Borgia, the Queen of Sheba, and Cleopatra as possible lovers. They tempt him, but to no avail. Faust and Marguerite declare their love for one another, Marguerite claiming that the bargain with Mephisto will not stand. She will marry Faust and take him away from Mephisto. The marriage is performed in Hell, with Lucifer presiding and Mephisto as best man. When Lucifer asks if there are any impediments to the marriage, Mulciber, one of Mephisto's aides, produces a baby. Marguerite admits it is her child; then, with fitting violin music, she tells a very sentimental story of how she was betrayed by a man she was trying to reform. At the close of the marriage ceremony, while Faust and Marguerite are being congratulated, Mephisto and Mulciber attempt to sneak the baby out of Hell so that it will avoid infant damnation for not having been baptized. However, the big pink ear appears at the window and they know it is too late. The concluding line, spoken by Mephisto, suggests the still unresolved conflict over the presence of evil in the world and the irrationality of some divine acts: "I'd rather live in Hell myself than be one of the outfit that *sends* people here for things they can't help" (CFO, 314).

Marquis makes a serious point in this absurd skit. There is no way to avoid Jehovah's judgment—whether merciful or not. Mephisto will try to alleviate suffering for those who are innocent, but his definition of "innocent" does not always correspond with the definition implied by the big pink ear.

It is tempting to draw a parallel between this skit and *The Adding Machine,* an earlier drama by Elmer Rice, which presents a mechanical man in a predetermined world. True, Mr. Zero is allowed to return to earth over and over, but always at the bottom. He will never have any freedom, nor does he want any. The final line of that play, spoken by a character similar to Mephisto, is even more negative than Mephisto's view: Lt. Charles, the Mephisto-like character, is referring to his job of sending souls back to earth to live in yet one more body when he says, "Hell, I'll tell the world this is a lousy job!"[8]

All in all, Marquis presents a rather simple view of man's relationship to God. He sees God as being rather irrational, acting from motives mankind cannot appreciate. As man grows more sophisticated, his view of God will also grow and he will have less need of a personal god. Jesus is seen as the Son of God; his solution to man's problems is love and kindness. Yet, instead of accepting these rather simple virtues, men have concentrated on Christ's miracles or the threat he represents to those less idealistic than he.

Finally, like Mark Twain, Marquis drew on the man-God relationship for his most effective work. Parts of *Chapters for the Orthodox* are Marquis at his best. Like Twain, he uses the Old Testament comically; however, he also uses parts of the New Testament in similar fashion. He freely presents his concept of Heaven and Hell, of God and the Devil. Like Twain, Marquis was troubled by the inconsistencies between free will and predestination, between a supposedly loving God and the immense cruelty of the world created by God. Nowhere in his work does Marquis reach the level of Twain's bitterness in *The Mysterious Stranger;* neither does he reach the level of artistry demonstrated by Twain in dealing with similar questions in *Huck Finn.* However, parts of *Chapters for the Orthodox* are Marquis at his best.

CHAPTER 11

"Is the Stuff Literature?"[1]

I   *The Paradox of Popularity*

AT present, there is no Don Marquis revival, nor does one seem likely. The majority of his published works are out of print, and to those accustomed to the humor of Donald Barthelme and John Barth, much of Marquis's humor would be dated. It would be a disservice to Don Marquis to insist on his being a great American writer. Undoubtedly, *Archy and Mehitabel* will survive; however, very few of Marquis's nonhumorous poems, stories, novels, and plays have stood the test of time; possibly none of them deserves to. The simple fact is that Marquis was very uneven. At best, he could leave pages that are as fresh as the day Archy or The Old Soak "wrote" them. Marquis's friends, such as Christopher Morley, excused his weaker work by claiming he wrote it under extreme economic pressure and was destroyed by overwork.[2] Certainly, Marquis did face heavy financial responsibilities; yet, they were no heavier than those faced by other writers. Others have excused his poorer work as being produced under the pressure of a newspaper or magazine deadline. However, at least one close friend believed Marquis worked best in a tumultuous setting.[3]

I do believe that without his ventures into nonhumorous writing, Marquis would not have been so successful as a humorist. As the previous chapters have demonstrated, the same themes turn up in both his humorous and nonhumorous work: the question of reincarnation, human vanity, man's belief, the value of the artist, individualism, the need for love, the need for freedom, man's cruelty to man. While these are not at all original with Marquis, he does use them very well in his best work.

II   *The Twain Connection*

As I have mentioned at various times throughout this book, when reading Don Marquis, it is very easy to link him with Mark Twain—

to see him as a "Son of Mark," which, given Marquis's birthdate, could have been literally true under different circumstances. While it may seem ridiculous or insignificant today, during Marquis's lifetime such a comparison was taken seriously, most seriously by Christopher Morley, Marquis's greatest champion. On June 2, 1937, approximately six months before Marquis's death, Morley delivered the annual Avery Hopwood Lecture at the University of Michigan. Entitled "A Successor to Mark Twain," the lecture makes a determined case for Marquis as ". . . our closest spiritual descendant of Mark Twain."[4] Morley begins by showing similarities in the two humorists' early background, their lack of formal education, and similarities in subject matter. However, much of the lecture is given over to a summary of Marquis's career, with emphasis on the difficulty of producing good work as a newspaper reporter.

Then, near the conclusion of the lecture, Morley, in a paragraph, sums up the parallels he sees between Mark Twain and Don Marquis:

Briefly to recapitulate . . . the lines of parallelism where you will find in Marquis and Mark Twain temperamental affinity. You will observe it in their fundamental comedian's instinct to turn suddenly without warning from the beautiful to the grotesque, or vice versa. You will find it in a rich vein of anger and disgust, turning on the genteel and cruel hypocrisies with the fury of a child or an archangel. You will find it in a kindly and respectful charity to the underdog: they are both infracaninophiles. You will find it in their passionate interest in religion and philosophy—with which is joined a blandly mischievous delight in shocking those for whom shocking is good. You will find it . . . in their habitual employment of a devastating Anglo-Saxonism of speech and epithet. And finally you'll observe that both had a keen (and somewhat ham) dramatic sense, which Marquis expressed in plays and Mark Twain in his superlative performances on the lecture platform.[5]

Morley goes on to even claim Marquis is a much greater poet than Mark Twain, a claim not so overwhelming to those who have read Twain's poetry.

Brushing aside the obvious similarities, how much of what Morley says still holds true? And what difference does it make? Actually, it is doubtful that Marquis's best work was written under the direct influence of Twain. The most obvious influence of Twain is in *Danny's Own Story* and this is hardly Marquis at his best.

It would be unusual if two American humorists growing up in similar environments in the same rough time span did not use similar subject matter and techniques. What is of more interest is what Morley may have meant by calling Marquis "our closest spiritual descendant of Mark Twain." Most of what Marquis says about mankind and its behavior can be found somewhere in Twain. Like Twain, Marquis was suspicious of institutional religion, but was interested in the Bible. He saw man as being foolish, weak, irrational, and cruel; yet he also saw man as capable of kindness, faith, and, although less probable, intelligent action. Marquis is more optimistic than Twain about mankind, never reaching the bitterness of *The Mysterious Stranger*.

Finally, whether or not Marquis is a "Son of Mark" is not the crucial question when making a final evaluation of Marquis as a humorist. Whether he consciously or unconsciously relied on Twain, George Ade, Joel Chandler Harris, or other American humorists, the real question is how good is Marquis's humor? How well has it survived the passage of time?

III   *What the Critics Are Saying*

With the exception of Edward Anthony's largely uncritical *O Rare Don Marquis* (1962), Marquis has received little critical attention since his death in 1937. Walter Blair discusses him briefly in *Native American Humor*. In fairness, it must be added that Blair and Hamlin Hill devote considerable space to Marquis in their study of American humor from *Poor Richard* to *Doonesbury*. They are particularly good at linking Marquis with other humorists. Norris Yates's chapter on Marquis in his study of modern American humor (1964) is very good on Archy and Mehitabel. Yates also explores Marquis's versatility and has some interesting comments about *The Almost Perfect State*. Louis Hasley's 1971 article on Marquis takes a realistic view of Marquis's work. In a few pages, he distinguishes clearly between the work that should still be read and that part of Marquis's work that should be forgotten.

Not surprisingly, E. B. White's introduction to the one-volume anthology of the three Archy and Mehitabel books, published by Doubleday in 1950, is the single most sensitive critical treatment of Don Marquis. As a fellow humorist, White understands the price Marquis paid for his creativity. Christopher Morley, Marquis's greatest champion, also celebrated the publication of the trilogy in an article that is, predictably, highly reminiscent, but does make some interesting observations about the origin of Archy. Morley also places considerable emphasis on Marquis's intense desire for recognition as a great writer.

A little later, in 1955, Bernard DeVoto paid tribute to Marquis. He used an essay, written when he was in charge of "The Easy Chair" in *Harper's*, to rebuke those who had never heard of Marquis and had relegated him to the ranks of forgotten humorists. Other articles by contemporaries of Marquis such as Chester Crowell (1946) and Rollin Kirby (1947) are largely anecdotal, although Kirby does place considerable emphasis on Marquis's poetic ability. Finally, in 1967, Corey Ford, a fellow humorist and friend of Marquis, devoted considerable space to Marquis in *The Time of Laughter*. Placing Marquis in the framework of the early twentieth century, Ford puts him at the top of American humor.

When Edward Anthony's *O Rare Don Marquis* was published in 1962, the stage might have been set for a Marquis revival. One never took place. Certainly, the biography did attract attention, some of it negative. In fairness to Anthony, he never claimed to have written a critical study of Marquis's work. What he does give the reader is a very affectionate portrait of Marquis the man, supported by a reprinting of much primary and secondary material not readily available elsewhere. Marquis had already been used by other friends in their autobiographies: George Middleton, in 1947, described his friendship with Marquis in Hollywood; in 1949, Charles Baynes, who had known Marquis well in Atlanta, wrote fondly of him. In 1954, Grantland Rice described his close friendship with Marquis when they were newspapermen in Atlanta and, later, when Marquis had become a famous humorist and Rice had become the best-known sportswriter in the United States.

For those interested in actually reading Marquis, the Doubleday edition of *Archy and Mehitabel* is still available. There is also a paperback edition of *Archy and Mehitabel*. A number of his other books are available in reprint editions;[6] however, none of these is likely to be available to the general public. Marquis has been included in various anthologies.[7] While it is foolish to believe that, if more of Marquis's work were available in less expensive editions, he would be more widely known and would have a better reputation, it is equally foolish to deny the possibility.

IV *"Is the Stuff Literature?"*

By using the word "stuff" in referring to Marquis's work, Morley takes a deliberately lowbrow attitude, almost as if he can sense the critical neglect that would be Marquis's fate in the years after his death. Yet, as mentioned before, the greatest disservice one could do Marquis would be to insist that everything he wrote was great or even good. Like Twain, he produced a great deal of inferior work and a small amount of very good work.

Whether Marquis is a minor major humorist or a major minor humorist or, as I believe, a major American humorist is unimportant. He will never, I suspect, be put on a level with Thurber, Perelman, Benchley, or E. B. White, although, at his best, he was certainly their equal.

Archy and Mehitabel will stay in print. Some of his other works have been reprinted during the past few years; however, it is highly unlikely that he will ever again reach a mass audience or even a very large audience. Yet, he will always find an appreciative audience— even if it is the small one for whom, as E. B. White put it, Marquis's humor will be " . . . full of sad beauty, bawdy adventure, political wisdom, and wild surmise; full of pain and jollity, full of exact and inspired writing."[8]

Notes and References

Chapter One

1. Stuart P. Sherman, "Don Marquis—What Is He?" *New York Herald Tribune Books*, 8 Feb. 1925, p. 1.
2. Edward Anthony, *O Rare Don Marquis* (Garden City, N.Y.: Doubleday, 1962), p. 411. I am indebted to Anthony's biography for much of the factual information contained in his book. Only direct quotations will be cited in the text.
3. Don Marquis, *The Best of Don Marquis*, ed. Christopher Morley (Garden City, N.Y.: Doubleday, 1946).
4. Bernard DeVoto, "Almost Toujour Gai," in *The Easy Chair* (Boston: Houghton Mifflin, 1955), pp. 65–73; and E. B. White, "Don Marquis," in *The Second Tree From the Corner* (New York: Harper and Brothers, 1954), pp. 182–89.
5. *Walnut Centennial Book* (Walnut, Illinois, 1972).
6. Don Marquis, "Confessions of a Reformed Columnist," *Saturday Evening Post*, 22 Dec. 1928, p. 6.
7. Ibid., p. 6.
8. Hamlin Hill, "Archy and Uncle Remus: Don Marquis's Debt to Joel Chandler Harris," *Georgia Review* 15 (Spring 1961): 80.
9. Ibid., p. 80.
10. Franklin Pierce Adams, known as F.P.A., wrote "The Conning Tower," probably the most influential daily column being published in New York during Marquis's early years there.
11. *Her Foot Is on the Brass Rail;* "An Ode to Hollywood"; *Mr. Hawley Breaks into Song.*
12. George Middleton, *These Things Are Mine* (New York: Macmillan, 1947), pp. 391–92.
13. Ibid., p. 391.
14. Ibid.
15. Benjamin DeCasseres, *Don Marquis* (New York: n.p., 1938), p. 371.
16. Ibid., p. 8.
17. Ibid.
18. Ibid., p. 12.
19. Ibid.
20. Ibid.

Chapter Two

1. Don Marquis, "Confessions of a Reformed Columnist," *Saturday Evening Post*, 29 Dec. 1928, p. 62.
2. Don Marquis, "Confessions," 22 Dec. 1928, p. 6.
3. Marquis, "Confessions," 29 Dec. 1928, p. 60.
4. Marquis, "Confessions," 22 Dec. 1928, p. 53.
5. Carl Van Doren, "Day In and Day Out," *Century* 70 (December 1923): 313.
6. Don Marquis, "The Lantern," *New York Herald Tribune*, 15 May 1924, p. 14.
7. Ibid.
8. Don Marquis, "The Lantern," 26 April 1924, p. 12.
9. Ibid.
10. Bruce Bliven, "Tempest Over Teapot," *American Heritage* 16 (August 1965): 21.
11. Don Marquis, "The Lantern," 10 June 1924, p. 14.
12. Don Marquis, "The Lantern," 1 May 1924, p. 12.
13. Ibid.
14. Don Marquis, "The Lantern," 13 June 1924, p. 12.
15. Ibid.
16. Don Marquis, "The Lantern," 19 March 1924, p. 14.
17. Don Marquis, "The Lantern," 27 March 1924, p. 12.
18. Ibid.
19. Ibid.
20. Ibid.
21. Ibid.
22. Ibid.
23. Don Marquis, "What Happens to Grouches," *Collier's*, 8 April 1933, p. 28.
24. Ibid.
25. Don Marquis, "If You Know What I Mean," *Collier's*, 9 January 1926, p. 18.
26. Ibid.
27. Ibid.
28. E. B. White, "Don Marquis," in *The Second Tree from the Corner* (New York: Harper and Brothers, 1954), pp. 188–89.

Chapter Three

1. Don Marquis, *The Lives and Times of Archy and Mehitabel* (Garden City, N.Y.: Doubleday, 1950). All further references to this work will be cited in the text.

2. Quoted in Hamlin Hill, "Archy and Uncle Remus: Don Marquis's Debt to Joel Chandler Harris," *Georgia Review* 15 (Spring 1961): 80.
3. Ibid., p. 81.
4. E. B. White, "Don Marquis," in *The Second Tree from the Corner* (New York: Harper and Brothers, 1954), p. 184.
5. Mehitabel was further immortalized in 1954 when Carol Channing portrayed the indestructible feline on a recording of a jazz opera of *Archy and Mehitabel* that had been performed earlier that year in New York, with Eddie Bracken playing Archy. In 1957, "Shinbone Alley," another musical version of *Archy and Mehitabel*, with Eartha Kitt as Mehitabel and Eddie Bracken again playing Archy, had a short run on Broadway. One other person who added a great deal to the success of *Archy and Mehitabel* must be mentioned. George Herriman, the creator of *Krazy Kat*, illustrated the three Archy and Mehitabel books, creating the perfect visual background for Archy's poetry.
6. White, p. 186.

Chapter Four

1. Louis Hasley, "Don Marquis: Ambivalent Humorist," *Prairie Schooner* 45 (Spring 1971): 59.
2. Ibid., p. 62.
3. Ibid., p. 66.
4. Don Marquis, *The Old Soak* (Garden City, N.Y.: Sun Dial Press, 1937), p. 5. All further references to *The Old Soak*, except for the dramatic version, in this chapter are to this edition.
5. Andrew Sinclair, *Era of Excess* (New York: Harper and Row, 1964), pp. 182–90.
6. Don Marquis, *The Old Soak's History of the World* (Garden City, N.Y.: Doubleday, 1937), p. 60. All further references to *The Old Soak's History of the World* in this chapter are to this edition.
7. The three stories are "When the Turtles Sing," "The Well," and "In the Bulrushes."
8. Alexander Woollcott, "Don Marquis's Hero," *New York Times*, 23 Aug. 1922, p. 14.
9. Don Marquis, *The Old Soak* (New York: Samuel French, 1926), p. 33.
10. Ibid., pp. 69–70.
11. Ibid., pp. 83–84.
12. Two movies were made of *The Old Soak*. One, a silent film released in 1926, was "transformed into a melodramatic morality play about the evils of drink" (Anthony, 432). In 1937 a talking version called *The Good Old Soak*, starring Wallace Beery, was released. Marquis had a special showing in his home, and the movie was much better received than the silent version.

However, the character of The Old Soak was softened, evidently to fit Beery's image (Anthony, 633–35).

13. Don Marquis, *Hermione and Her Little Group of Serious Thinkers* (New York: D. Appleton & Co., 1916), p. 1. All further references to *Hermione* in this chapter are to this edition.

14. "Don Marquis's Brilliant Satire on Intellectual Fads and Freaks of Today," *Current Opinion* 62 (January 1917): 47.

15. *Current Opinion*, p. 47.

16. Bernard DeVoto, "Almost Toujour Gai," in *The Easy Chair* (Boston: Houghton Mifflin, 1955), p. 69.

17. Norris Yates, "The Many Masks of Don Marquis," in *The American Humorist: Conscience of the Twentieth Century* (Ames: Iowa State Univ. Press, 1964), pp. 212–13.

18. Hasley, p. 67.

19. Don Marquis, "Hermione the Bolshevik," *Outlook* 23 (July 1919): 482.

Chapter Five

1. One can find this view stated by nearly everyone who writes about Marquis: E. B. White, Christopher Morley, and Louis Hasley, among others.

2. David McCord, "Introduction," *What Cheer* (New York: Random House, 1955), p. xliii.

3. Ibid.

4. Don Marquis, "The Jesters," in *Dreams and Dust* (New York: Harper and Brothers, 1915), pp. 129–31.

5. Don Marquis, "The Jesters" in *The Awakening*, New York: Doubleday, Page & Co., 1920, p. 67.

6. Ibid.

7. Ibid., p. 68.

8. Don Marquis, "The Tavern of Despair," in *Dreams and Dust*, p. 67.

9. Don Marquis, "Improbably Epitaphs," *Noah an' Jonah an' Cap'n John Smith* (New York: Appleton, 1921), pp. 34–35.

10. Don Marquis, "Proverbs xii, 7," in *Noah an' Jonah an' Cap'n John Smith*, p. 33.

11. Don Marquis, "Old Titian Loved Your Sort of Fiery Mop," in *Sonnets to a Red-Haired Lady . . . and Famous Love Affairs* (Garden City, N.Y.: Doubleday, 1922), p. 3.

12. Don Marquis, "Phyllida," in *The Awakening*, p. 96.

13. Don Marquis, "Pedder," in *Poems and Portraits* (Garden City, N.Y.: Doubleday, 1922), p. 132.

14. Don Marquis, "An Ancient Souvenir," in *Love Sonnets of a Caveman and Other Poems* (Garden City, N.Y.: Doubleday, 1928), p. 16.

15. Don Marquis, "Adam and Eve," in *Sonnets to a Red-Haired Lady . . . and Famous Love Affairs*, p. 121.

16. Don Marquis, "Petrarch and Laura," in *Sonnets to a Red-Haired Lady ... and Famous Love Affairs*, p. 108.
17. Don Marquis, "Down in a Wine Vault," in *The Old Soak and Hail and Farewell* (Garden City, N.Y.: Doubleday, 1921), p. 100.
18. Ibid., p. 102.
19. Ibid.
20. Don Marquis, "Noah an' Jonah an' Cap'n John Smith," in *The Old Soak and Hail and Farewell*, p. 146.
21. Ibid., pp. 147–48.
22. Ibid., pp. 150–51.
23. Don Marquis, "The God-Maker, Man," in *The Awakening*, p. 28.
24. Don Marquis, "New York," in *The Awakening*, p. 13.
25. Don Marquis, "Proem," in *Dreams and Dust*, p. ix.
26. Don Marquis, "A Gentleman of Fifty Soliloquizes," in *The Awakening*, pp. 60–61.

Chapter Six

1. Don Marquis, *Danny's Own Story* (Garden City, N.Y.: Doubleday, 1912), p. 126.
2. Ibid., p. 87.
3. Ibid., pp. 185–86.
4. Ibid., p. 264.
5. Ibid., p. 285.
6. Ibid., p. 333.
7. Christopher Morley, "A Successor to Mark Twain," in *Letters of Askance* (Philadelphia: J. B. Lippincott Company, 1939), p. 86.
8. Marquis dedicated *The Cruise of the Jasper B.* to copyreaders.
9. Don Marquis, *The Cruise of the Jasper B.* (New York: D. Appleton & Co., 1916), p. 16.
10. Ibid., p. 200.
11. Ibid., pp. 277–79.
12. Don Marquis, *Off the Arm* (Garden City, N.Y.: Doubleday, 1930), pp. 5–6.
13. Ibid., p. 205.
14. Louis Hasley, "Don Marquis, Ambivaient Humorist," Prairie Schooner 45 (Spring 1971): 59, p. 65.
15. Henry S. Canby, "Unfinished Symphony," *Saturday Review of Literature*, 18 Feb. 1939, p. 7.
16. Stanley Young, "The Last Work of Don Marquis," *New York Times Book Review*, 19 Feb. 1939, p. 6.
17. Isabel Patterson, "Son of the Small Town," *New York Herald Tribune Books*, 19 Feb. 1939, p. 4.

18. Don Marquis, *Sons of the Puritans* (Garden City, N.Y.: Doubleday, 1939), p. 34.

19. Christopher Morley, "Preface," *Sons of the Puritans,* pp. v–vi.

Chapter Seven

1. The use of the frame in early American humor is described by Walter Blair in *Native American Humor* (San Francisco: Chandler, 1960), pp. 90–102.

2. Don Marquis, "Rooney's Touchdown," in *The Revolt of the Oyster* (Garden City, N.Y.: Doubleday, 1922), p. 65.

3. Ibid., p. 72.

4. Ibid., p. 77.

5. Ibid.

6. Don Marquis, "The Saddest Man," in *Sun Dial Time* (Garden City, NY..: Doubleday, 1936), p. 247.

7. Ibid., p. 273.

8. Marquis, "The Ancient Mariner," in *Sun Dial Time,* pp. 20–21.

9. Ibid., p. 34.

10. Ibid., pp. 19–20.

11. Don Marquis, "The Glass Eater's Story," in *A Variety of People* (Garden City, N.Y.: Doubleday, 1929), p. 316.

12. Don Marquis, "Country Doctor," in *The Best of Don Marquis,* ed. Christopher Morley (Garden City, N.Y.: Doubleday, 1946), pp. 444–64.

13. Don Marquis, "The Strong Grasses," in *A Variety of People,* pp. 3–24.

14. Don Marquis, "The Magic Melody," in *A Variety of People,* p. 298.

15. Don Marquis, "Carter," in *Carter and Other People* (New York: D. Appleton & Co., 1921), p. 8.

16. Ibid., p. 10.

17. Ibid.

18. Ibid., p. 15.

19. Ibid., p. 17.

Chapter Eight

1. Don Marquis, "Stage-Struck," *Saturday Evening Post,* 8 March 1930, p. 78.

2. Ibid.

3. Don Marquis, *The Dark Hours* (New York: Doubleday, 1924), p. 152.

4. Ibid., pp. 153–54.

5. Ibid., p. 23.

6. Ibid., p. 28.

7. Joseph Wood Krutch, "Passion Play," *Nation,* 30 (November 1932): 452.

8. *Brewer's Dictionary of Phrase and Fable* (New York: Harper and Brothers, n.d.), p. 919.
9. Don Marquis, *Out of the Sea*, pp. 132–33.
10. Don Marquis, *Master of the Revels* (Garden City, N.Y.: Doubleday, 1934), pp. 239–42.
11. *Book Review Digest*, 1934, p. 615.
12. Marquis, *Master of the Revels*, p. 242.
13. Ibid., pp. 76–78.
14. Ibid., p. 234.

Chapter Nine

1. Bernard DeVoto, "Almost Toujours Gai," in *The Easy Chair* (Boston: Houghton Mifflin, 1955), p. 68.
2. Don Marquis, *Prefaces* (New York: D. Appleton Co., 1919). All other references to *Prefaces* in this chapter are to this edition.
3. DeVoto, pp. 65–66.
4. Thomas Masson, "Don Marquis," in *Our American Humorists* (Freeport, N.Y.: Books for Libraries, 1966), p. 259.
5. Christopher Morley, "A Successor to Mark Twain," in *Letters of Askance* (Philadelphia: J. B. Lippincott Company, 1939), pp. 104–105.
6. Don Marquis, *The Almost Perfect State* (Garden City, N.Y.: Doubleday, 1927), pp. 3–4. All further references to *The Almost Perfect State* in this chapter are to this edition.
7. Morley, p. 116.
8. Louis Hasley, "Don Marquis: Ambivalent Humorist," *Prairie Schooner* 45 (Spring 1971): 67–68.
9. DeVoto, p. 68.
10. Norris Yates, "The Many Masks of Don Marquis," in *The American Humorist: Conscience of the Twentieth Century*, pp. 209–10.
11. Ibid.
12. Ibid., p. 211.
13. Ibid.
14. Thomas Jefferson, "Letter to John Adams, Oct. 28, 1813," in *The Portable Thomas Jefferson*, ed. Merrill C. Peterson (New York: Viking, 1975), p. 534.
15. Ibid., pp. 534–35.
16. Ibid., p. 535.
17. Thomas Jefferson, *Notes on the State of Virginia* (New York: Harper and Row, 1964), p. 158.
18. Yates, p. 210.
19. Elmer Rice, "The Adding Machine," in *Twentieth Century American Writing*, ed. William T. Stafford (New York: Odyssey Press, 1965), p. 340.

Chapter Ten

1. Christopher Morley, "A Successor to Mark Twain," in *Letters of Askance* (Philadelphia: J. B. Lippincott Company, 1939), p. 105.
2. Don Marquis, *The Old Soak's History of the World* (Garden City, N.Y.: Sun Dial Press, 1937), p. 16.
3. Don Marquis, *Prefaces*, p. 149.
4. Don Marquis, "The God-Maker Man," in *The Awakening*, p. 28.
5. Don Marquis, "Do You Believe in a Future Life?" *American Magazine* 216 (November 1933): 105.
6. Don Marquis, *Chapters for the Orthodox* (Garden City, N.Y.: Doubleday, 1934), p. vi. All further references to *Chapters for the Orthodox* in this chapter are to this edition.
7. Don Marquis, "Three Pigs," *Harper's* 140 (December 1919): 137–38.
8. Elmer Rice, "The Adding Machine," p. 347.

Chapter Eleven

1. Don Marquis, *The Lives and Times of Archy and Mehitabel* (Garden City, N.Y.: Doubleday, 1950), p. 22.
2. Christopher Morley, "O Rare Don Marquis," in *Letters of Askance* (Philadelphia: J. B. Lippincott Company, 1939), pp. 117–18.
3. Rollin Kirby, "Don Marquis: Delayed Elizabethan," *American Mercury* 64 (March 1947): 337–38.
4. Christopher Morley, "A Successor to Mark Twain," in *Letters of Askance*, p. 83.
5. Ibid.
6. Books for Libraries Press, Freeport, New York, reprinted *Carter and Other People, Sun Dial Time,* and *When the Turtle Sings* in 1970. At present, Microfilms International has the following Marquis works available: *The Almost Perfect State, The Best of Don Marquis, The Cruise of the Jasper B., Love Sonnets of a Cave Man and Other Verses, Master of the Revels, The Old Soak and Hail and Farewell, Prefaces, Sons of the Puritans, A Variety of People,* and *Words and Thoughts.*
7. Marquis has been included in a number of anthologies of American humors and popular culture. The following are representative: *The American Twenties,* ed. John K. Hutchens (New York, 1972): reprints "The Song of Mehitabel." *The Jazz Age,* ed. Max Bogart (New York, 1969): reprints "Certain Maxims of Archy." *A Subtreasury of American Humor,* ed. E. B. and Katherine White (New York, 1941): reprints a Marquis fable, some of the *Sonnets to a Red-Haired Lady,* and several selections from *Archy and Mehitabel.*
8. E. B. White, "Don Marquis," in *The Second Tree From the Corner* (New York: Harper and Brothers, 1954), p. 185.

Selected Bibliography

PRIMARY SOURCES

1. Books by Marquis
The Almost Perfect State. Garden City, New York: Doubleday, Page & Co., 1927.
The Awakening. Garden City, New York: Doubleday, Page & Co., 1925.
The Best of Don Marquis. ed. Christopher Morley. Garden City, New York: Doubleday & Co., 1946.
Carter and Other People. New York: D. Appleton & Co., 1921.
Chapters for the Orthodox. Garden City, New York: Doubleday, Doran & Co., 1934.
The Cruise of the Jasper B. New York: D. Appleton & Co., 1916.
Danny's Own Story. Garden City, New York: Doubleday, Page & Co., 1912.
The Dark Hours. New York: Doubleday, Page & Co., 1924.
Dreams and Dust. New York: Harper and Brothers, 1915.
Everything's Jake. Tacoma, Washington: Non-Profit Press, 1978.
Her Foot Is on the Brass Rail. New York: The Marchbanks Press, 1935.
Hermione and Her Little Group of Serious Thinkers. New York: D. Appleton & Co., 1916.
Lives and Times of Archy and Mehitabel, The. "Introduction" by E. B. White. Garden City, New York: Doubleday & Co., 1950.
Love Sonnets of a Caveman and Other Poems. Garden City, New York: Doubleday, Doran & Co., 1928.
Master of the Revels. Garden City, New York: Doubleday, Doran & Co., 1934.
Noah an' Jonah an' Cap'n John Smith. New York: D. Appleton & Co., 1921.
Off the Arm. Garden City, New York: Doubleday, Doran & Co., 1930.
Old Soak, The. Garden City, New York: The Sun Dial Press, 1937.
Old Soak, The. New York: Samuel French, 1926.
Old Soak and Hail and Farewell, The. Garden City, New York: Doubleday, Doran & Co., The Sun Dial Press, 1937.
Old Soak's History of the World, The. Garden City, New York: The Sun Dial Press, 1937.
Out of the Sea. Garden City, New York: Doubleday, Page & Co., 1927.
Poems and Portraits. New York: Doubleday, Page & Co., 1922.
Prefaces. New York: D. Appleton & Co., 1919.
Revolt of the Oyster, The. Garden City, New York: Doubleday, Page & Co., 1922.

Sonnets to a Red-Haired Lady . . . and Famous Love Affairs. Garden City,
New York: Doubleday, Page & Co., 1922.
Sons of the Puritans. Garden City, New York: Doubleday, Doran & Co.,
1939.
Sun Dial Time. Garden City, New York: Doubleday, Doran & Co., 1936.
Variety of People, A. Garden City, New York: Doubleday, Doran & Co.,
1929.
When the Turtles Sing. Garden City, New York: Doubleday, Doran & Co.,
1928.

2. Selected Unreprinted Pieces by Marquis (exclusive of unreprinted material from "The Sun Dial" and "The Lantern")

"All the Answers." *Collier's,* 1 July 1933, p. 28.
"Among the Young." *Collier's,* 14 Jan. 1933, p. 32.
"Are You Ready to Swear Off in January?" *American Magazine* 93 (January
1922): 8–9. 56–58.
"Autobiographies." *Saturday Evening Post,* 17 May 1930, pp. 42, 58.
"Being a Public Character." *American Magazine* 84 (Sept. 1917): 19–23, 68.
"Blood Will Tell." *American Magazine* 80 (November 1915): 5–9.
"Blow the Trumpet! Beat the Drum!" *Forum* 80 (December 1928): 581–84.
"Busy Bolshevism." *Collier's,* 29 Aug. 1931, pp. 30, 45.
"Confessions of a Reformed Columnist." *Saturday Evening Post,* 22 Dec.
1928, pp. 6–7, 53. Part II of this article is in the *Saturday Evening Post,*
29 Dec. 1928, pp. 59–60, 62.
"Crime Situation, The." *Collier's,* 28 Nov. 1931, pp. 19, 45.
"Don Marquis, by Himself." *Everybody's Magazine* 42 (January 1920): 29,
85.
"Do You Believe in a Future Life?" *American Magazine* 216 (November
1933): 30–31, 104.
"Eat, Drink, and Be Merry—For To-morrow Ye Diet." *American Magazine*
92 (October 1921): 7–9, 64.
"First Intelligible Answer, The." *Art World* 2 (May 1917): 166.
"Fits and Starts." *Harper's Magazine* 139 (July 1919): 277–79.
"Hermoine the Bolshevik." *Outlook,* 23 July 1919, p. 482.
"If You Know What I Mean." *Collier's,* 9 Jan. 1926, p. 18.
"In a Fair Way to Murder." *Collier's,* 16 April 1927, pp. 12, 36.
"Into the Literary Big Time." *Bookman* 49 (June 1919): 405–408.
"King O'Meara and Queen Guinevere." *Saturday Evening Post,* 15 March
1930, pp. 6–7, 146, 149, and 22 March 1930, pp. 22–23, 110, 114, 119,
121, 152, 154, 156.
"King's Job, A." *Collier's,* 7 July 1928, p. 13.
"McDermott and the War." *Everybody's Magazine* 39 (October 1918): 20–
24, 77–78.

"Mother Goose, Propagandist." *Harper's Magazine* 139 (August 1919): 439–40.

"My Memories of the Old-Fashioned Drummer." *American Magazine* 107 (February 1929): 20–21, 152–54.

"No Matter What They Think." *Collier's*, 7 Feb. 1931, pp. 11–13, 54, 56.

"O'Meara at Troy." *Saturday Evening Post*, 21 June 1930, pp. 18–19, 91, 93, 95.

"On Being Fifty-Five." *Harper's Magazine* 168 (Febuary 1934): 353–56.

"Other Woman, The." *Collier's*, 13 Dec. 1930, pp. 14–15, 44.

"Plight of a President, The." *Collier's*, 10 Dec. 1932, p. 17.

"Rise of Melisande Meringue, The." *Bookman* 49 (July 1919): 560–63.

"She Tells the Reporter." *Collier's*, 12 July 1930, p. 28.

"So the King Stopped It." *Collier's*, 21 July 1934, pp. 16, 43.

"Stage Struck." *Saturday Evening Post*, 8 March 1930, pp. 78, 81.

"Ten Minutes in a Barroom." *Collier's*, 19 Sept. 1931, pp. 21, 31.

"Ten Nights in a Drug Store." *Collier's*, 16 Sept. 1933, p. 26.

"There's Gold in Them Hills." *Collier's*, 7 Jan. 1928, p. 17.

"Three Pigs." *Harper's Magazine* 140 (December 1919): 137–38.

"What Happens to Grouches." *Collier's*, 8 April 1933, p. 28.

"What's the Matter with the Country?" *Collier's*, 22 Aug. 1931, p. 17.

"Whoop It Up!" *Collier's*, 7 Jan. 1933, p. 29.

"Wise Man's Wives, A." *Collier's*, 8 July 1933, p. 26.

"Your Aunt Emma." *American Magazine* 103 (June 1927): 66–67, 93.

"Your Cousin Mehitabel." *American Magazine* 106 (October 1928): 44–45, 112, 114.

"Your Uncle Ed." *American Magazine* 103 (May 1927): 26–27, 103–104.

SECONDARY SOURCES

ANON. *Book Review Digest*, 1934. Summaries of reviews of *Chapters for the Orthodox* and *Master of the Revels*.

―――. "The 'Column' Shaking," *Literary Digest*, 20 Sept. 1924, pp. 31–32. Marquis has announced he hates writing a column, and would like to give it up.

―――. "Don Marquis—American Minstrel." *Current Opinion* 73 (November 1922): 662–64. Marquis is a "full man," very human and humane.

―――. "Don Marquis Dies in His Home at 59." *New York Times*, 30 Dec. 1937, p. 19. Obituary which emphasizes Marquis's precarious financial condition and health problems. Praises Marquis as being a good poet who will be remembered for Archy and Mehitabel.

―――. "Don Marquis Preaches Courage." *Current Opinion* 78 (April 1925): 454–55. Praises Marquis, particularly *The Dark Hours*. Marquis has Gospel of Courage.

————. "Don Marquis's Brilliant Satire on Intellectual Fads and Freaks of Today." *Current Opinion* 62 (January 1917): 47–48. Review of *Hermione and Her Little Group of Serious Thinkers*.

————. "Elusive Spirit." *Newsweek*, 5 Feb. 1962, p. 84. Review of *O Rare Don Marquis*. Finds it too pedestrian to catch Marquis's personality.

————. "Goodbye Don." *New York Times*, 30 Dec. 1937, p. 18. Editorial with high praise for Marquis, who is seen as "an Elizabethan born out of his time."

————. "The Literary Spotlight: xxxli Don Marquis." *Bookman* 59 (July 1924): 539–43. A somewhat humorous article that sees Marquis as a moralist.

ANTHONY, EDWARD. "Don Marquis Revisited." *Columbia Library Columns* 12 (2): 3–12. Deals with Anthony's search for materials for Marquis biography.

————. *O Rare Don Marquis*. Garden City, New York: Doubleday & Co., Inc., 1962. The only full-length biography of Marquis.

BAYNE, CHARLES J. *The Coming of the Crow's Feet*. Atlanta: Tupper and Love, 1949. Describes Bayne's friendship with Marquis; reprints several letters from Marquis.

BIER, JESSE. *The Rise and Fall of American Humor*. New York: Holt, Rinehart and Winston, 1968. Has numerous references to Marquis which place him in the mainstream of American humor.

BLAIR, WALTER, and HILL, HAMLIN. *America's Humor: From Poor Richard to Doonesbury*. New York: Oxford University Press, 1978. Contains considerable discussion of Marquis, particularly in relationship to other humorists.

BLAIR, WALTER. *Native American Humor*. San Francisco: Chandler Publishing Company, 1960. Brief discussion of Marquis.

BLIVEN, BRUCE. "Tempest over Teapot." *American Heritage* 16 (August 1965): 20–23, 100–105. Discusses Teapot Dome scandal, which was used by Marquis in his columns.

CANBY, HENRY S. "Unfinished Symphony." *Saturday Review of Literature*, 18 Feb. 1939, p. 7. Highly favorable review of *Sons of the Puritans*.

CROWELL, CHESTER. "The Fun of Don Marquis." *Atlantic Monthly* 178 (November 1946): 129–31. Numerous anecdotes about Marquis which emphasize his sense of humor.

DeCASSERES, BENJAMIN. *Don Marquis*. New York: n.p., 1938. Privately printed memorial describing Marquis's reception in Heaven.

————. "Portraits En Brochette: Don Marquis." *Bookman* 73 (July 1931): 487–91. Sees Marquis as a storyteller like Twain, a bohemian like Whitman.

DeVOTO, BERNARD. "Almost Toujour Gai." *The Easy Chair*. Boston: Houghton Mifflin Company, 1955, pp. 65–73. Highly favorable discussion of Marquis as a humorist who should be more highly regarded than he is.

EDSON, C. L. *The Gentle Art of Columning.* New York: Brentano's, 1920. Has an introduction written by Marquis. Devotes most of a chapter to Marquis as a columnist with quotation from several columns.

FORD, COREY. *The Time of Laughter,* Boston: Little, Brown and Company, 1967. Places Marquis at the top of American humor. Has numerous anecdotes.

HAMBLEN, ABIGAIL ANN. "Protestantism in Three American Novels." *Forum* (Houston, Texas University) 3 (5): 40–43. Brief discussion of *Sons of the Puritans.* Tries to connect it with *The Scarlet Letter.*

HASLEY, LOUIS. "Don Marquis: Ambivalent Humorist." *Prairie Schooner* 45 (Spring 1971): 59–73. Good general survey of Marquis's major works.

HILL, HAMLIN. "Archy and Uncle Remus: Don Marquis's Debt to Joel Chandler Harris." *Georgia Review* 15 (Spring 1961): 78–87. Connects Uncle Remus stories to Archy and Mehitabel; also places Marquis firmly in the mainstream of American humor.

JAFFE, DAN. "Archy Jumps over the Moon." *The Twenties,* ed. Warren French. Deland, Florida: Everett/Edwards, Inc., 1975, pp. 427–37. Good parodies of Marquis.

JEFFERSON, THOMAS. *Notes on The State of Virginia.* New York: Harper and Row, 1964. Both works by Jefferson give background for Marquis's agrarianism, a view that he held throughout his career.

——. *The Portable Thomas Jefferson,* ed. Merril D. Peterson. New York: The Viking Press, 1975.

KIRBY, ROLLIN. "Don Marquis: Delayed Elizabethan." *American Mercury* 44 (March 1947): 337–40. Deals with Marquis's personality; sees him as a poet who touched the hem of greatness.

KRUTCH, JOSEPH WOOD. "Passion Play." *Nation,* 30 Nov. 1932, p. 542. Review of *The Dark Hours.*

MCCORD, DAVID. "Introduction." *What Cheer.* New York: Random House, 1955, pp. xxvii–xliv. Discusses the problems of writing good comic verse.

MASSON, THOMAS. *Our American Humorists.* Freeport, New York: Books for Libraries Press, Inc., 1966. Includes a chapter about Marquis which reprints some of his work.

MIDDLETON, GEORGE. *These Things Are Mine.* New York: Macmillan, 1947. Description of Marquis in Hollywood by a fellow writer.

MILLETT, FRED B. Review of *O Rare Don Marquis. American Literature* 35 (January 1964): 546–48. Millett doesn't think much of the biography; finds it "naive and artless."

MORLEY, CHRISTOPHER. "A Successor to Mark Twain" and "O Rare Don Marquis." *Letters of Askance.* Philadelphia: J. B. Lippincott Company, 1939. The first article makes the strongest case for Marquis being Twain's heir; the second is more personal, discussing Morley's close friendship with Marquis.

————. "Don Marquis: An Appreciation." *Tomorrow* 9 (May 1950): 52–53. Largely anecdotal, but stresses Marquis's intense ambition.

————. "Preface." *Sons of the Puritans.* Garden City, New York: Doubleday, Doran & Co., 1939. Suggests how Marquis might have finished the novel; describes Marquis's hopes for the novel.

PATTERSON, ISABEL. "Son of the Small Town." *New York Herald Tribune Books,* 19 Feb. 1939, p. 6. Favorable review of *Sons of the Puritans.*

RICE, ELMER. "The Adding Machine." *Twentieth Century American Writing,* ed. William T. Stafford. New York: The Odyessey Press, 1965, pp. 301–47. Marquis uses techniques and ideas highly similar to Rice in *Chapters For the Orthodox* and elsewhere.

RICE, GRANTLAND. *The Tumult and the Shouting.* New York: A. S. Barnes and Company, 1954. Rice describes his close friendship with Marquis during the latter's years in Atlanta.

SAYLER, OLIVE. "The Play of the Week." *Saturday Review of Literature,* 24 Dec. 1927, pp. 468–69. Review of *Out of the Sea.* Blames poor direction and poor acting for the play's lack of success.

SHERMAN, STUART B. "Don Marquis—What Is He?" *New York Herald Tribune Books,* 8 Feb. 1925, pp. 1–3. Sherman makes a good case for Marquis as primarily a poet. Reviews his work to 1925.

SINCLAIR, ANDREW. *Era of Excess.* New York: Harper and Row, 1964. A history of Prohibition, one of Marquis's greatest dislikes and favorite targets for humorous attack.

SPILLER, ROBERT E. et al., eds. *Literary History of the United States,* rev. ed. in one vol. New York: Macmillan, 1953, pp. 755, 1131. Emphasizes Marquis as columnist who created vivid comic characters.

STEADMAN, MARK SIDNEY, JR. *American Humor: 1920–1955.* Unpublished Ph.D. dissertation, Florida State University, 1963. Includes Marquis in discussions of characteristics of modern American humor.

STREETER, EDWARD. "Archie's Boss." *New York Times Book Review,* 4 Feb. 1962, p. 6. Review of *O Rare Don Marquis.*

THORP, WILLARD. *American Humorists.* Univ. of Minnesota pamphlets on American writers, no. 42. Minneapolis: Univ. of Minnesota Press, 1964. Brief mention of Marquis, with emphasis on his ability as a columnist.

TITTLE, W. "Glimpses of Interesting American." *Century* 110 (August 1925): 437–41. Interview with Marquis. Finds him humble and determined to become a successful playwright.

UPDIKE, JOHN. "Indignations of a Senior Citizen." *New York Times Book Review,* 25 Nov. 1962, p. 5. Review of James Thurber's *Credos and Curios* which rates Thurber as being less complex than Marquis or Benchley.

VAN DOREN, CARL. "Day In and Day Out." *Century* 70 (December 1923): 308–15. Favorable view of Marquis as columnist.

Walnut Centennial Book. Walnut, Illinois, 1972. Valuable for photographs and discussions of life in Walnut during Marquis's childhood.

WALTON, EDITH H. "Don Marquis's Story," *New York Times,* 22 Nov. 1936, sect. 7, p. 7. Favorable review of *Sun Dial Time.*

WHITE, E. B. "Don Marquis." *The Second Tree from the Corner.* New York: Harper and Brothers, 1954. A very sensitive appreciation of Marquis; also published as the introduction to *The Lives and Times of Archy and Mehitabel.*

WOOLLCOTT, ALEXANDER. "Don Marquis's Hero." *New York Times,* 23 Aug. 1922, p. 14. Favorable review of *The Old Soak.*

YATES, NORRIS. "The Many Masks of Don Marquis," in *The American Humorist: Conscience of the Twentieth Century.* Ames: Iowa State Univ. Press, 1964. Good discussion of Marquis, emphasizing his versatility. Yates is especially interesting in dealing with *Archy and Mehitabel.*

YOUNG, STANLEY. "The Last Work of Don Marquis." *New York Times Book Review,* 19 Feb. 1939, p. 6. Favorable review of *Sons of the Puritans.*

Index

Adams, Franklin P., 18, 25
Ade, George, 24, 116, 143
Anderson, Sherwood: *Winesburg, Ohio*, 91
Archy and Mehitabel: Archy's philosophy of life, 37–44; first appearance in "The Sun Dial," 19, 33–34; Marquis's view of Archy and Mehitabel, 32; Mehitabel's philosophy of life, 35–36
Atkinson, Brooks, 114

Barth, John, 141
Barthelme, Donald, 141
Bayne, Charles J., 114, 144
Benchley, Robert, 121, 145
Billings, Josh, 51
Blair, Walter, 143
Broun, Heywood, 25
Buchwald, Art, 27
Burroughs, John, 122

Calvin, John, 136, 137
Canby, Henry S., 88
Chaplin, Charlie, 88
Christian Science, 110, 127
Coburn, Charles, 114
Crowell, Chester, 144
Cuppy, Will, 122

Davis, Richard Harding, 83
DeCassares, Benjamin: *Don Marquis*, 22–23
DeVoto, Bernard, 15, 60, 117, 121–22, 144
Dooley, Martin, 51, 54–55
Dumas, Alexander, 83, 84

Eddy, Mary Baker, 127
Emerson, Ralph Waldo, 124, 124

Fairbanks, Douglas, 85, 88
Faulkner, William, 122
Field, Eugene, 24
Fields, W. C., 50, 74
Finch, Fothergil, 63–65
Fitzgerald, F. Scott; *The Last Tycoon*, 86
Ford, Corey, 144
Frost, Robert, 122

Hackett, Francis, 114
Hampden, Walter, 111
Harris, Joel Chandler, 17–18, 143
Hasley, Louis, 143
Hawley, Clem (The Old Soak), 19, 50–59, 126
Hermione, 19, 50, 59–66
Herriman, George, 149, ch.4, n.5
Hill, Hamlin, 18, 32–33, 143

Imagists, The, 63

Jefferson, Thomas, 122, 123–25
Jonson, Ben, 42, 43

Kemble, E. W., 80
Kipling, Rudyard, 48–49
Kirby, Rollin, 144
Krutch, Joseph Wood, 110–11

Laughton, Charles, 114
Lewis, Sinclair: *Main Street*, 91

McCutcheon, George Barr, 83
Marquis, Barbara, 20, 21
Marquis, Donald Robert Perry: attended Knox College, 16–17, 94; became successful columnist, 19; birth, 16; early childhood experiences, 16; early newspaper work, 17; free-lanced in

PS
3525   Lee, Lynn.
A67   Don Marquis
Z76